Bibliographic information of the German National Library: The German National Library lists this publication in the German National Bibliography; detailed bibliographic data are available on the Internet at http://dnb.dnb.de.

1st Edition June 2020 Original Edition

In parts this is a translation of the German book »Artgerechte Haltung von Menschen«.

Cover photo and design: Thomas Berg, Lübeck, www.bilderberg.tv

Production and publishing: BoD - Books on Demand, Norderstedt

ISBN 978-3-7519-0577-0

EDITION 99
»To the man who he will one day become«

Manuel Jork

The People Effect

The Art of Joining Forces to Unfold the Human
Potential

»I am not a self-made man. I've always treated the world as my classroom. Never stop learning. Ever. You know that wherever you are in life, there will be times when you don't have the answer, or drive, and you're forced to look beyond yourself. You can admit that you can't do it alone. I certainly can't. No one can.«

– Arnold Schwarzenegger
Foreword to »Tools of Titans« by Tim Ferris

Thinking and acting together, thus joining forces is my purpose for the near future. I do not distinguish between interactions of family, friends, neighbors, employees or colleagues. I address all people in all forms of relationships. I write equally for female and male readers and I also think of readers who feel different. I see the diversity and appreciate the equality. I'm just making it as easy as I can with the written language.

Foreword

In my own career, whether as an individual contributor, manager, leader, consultant, business owner, husband, father or member of my community, I have been very curious about how I can better work together with others for mutually beneficial outcomes. It can be hard at times. With the fast-paced world we seem to live in, at times it can seem daunting to consistently respect as well as create consistent cycles of value in the style preferences that exist between us. I'm talking about the sometimes-subtle preferences [often they just look like flat out differences] in how each of us like to do things, like: intensity of how we think, paying attention to details, the frequency and depth of our communication, the focus of when we learn, ability to tell jokes, how we respond to questions, the passion in how we express ourselves or the myriad of other style preferences that exist. This book tackles those style difference preferences and how to win together and achieve mutually beneficial outcomes. This book equips the reader to understand, value, and work with others to unlock the human potential amongst preference difference, both professionally and personally.

I met Manuel some time ago and have had the pleasure to witness him in action on numerous occasions. He is a master of the content, the principles and tools in this book. I have seen Manuel facilitate the tools in this book in the classroom, enabling workshop participants to understand the often-tricky dynamics of effectively communicating with others. I have witnessed Manuel use the skills offered here in going for win-win outcomes with clients and customers. He passes along the »how-to« in these book pages.

If you are willing to read, internalize and integrate the concepts in this book into your professional and personal life, you will see wiser outcomes. Manuel takes his decades of experience, learning, failures, trial and error and writes a masterpiece work allowing You and I to gain immense wisdom from his experience. This book will save you years of frustration that can sometimes accompany the always fluid dynamics of working and communicating with others.

You must however practice the tools offered in these pages to see to gain these skills. I consider myself very lucky to have crossed paths with Manuel and congratulate him on a well written book.

Enjoy the read!

– Kit Allowitz
Author of »Don't Pull the Chicken Switch: How to Maximize Willpower and Get Everything You Want Out of Work and Life«

Beware: There Comes Some Mind-Boggling Stuff

People have brains. It serves to unfold the potentials of human beings. Potentials are possibilities. People have an inexhaustible variety of possibilities. They are finely tuned creatures that are elastic and can withstand a lot. They are sensitive and empathic, they can reflect on themselves and others, they can transfer knowledge and experience to different fields of action and they can anticipate the effects of their actions. They can achieve great things with this.

But there's a catch.

No brain exists on its own. This sounds strange. Especially for individualists. But it's true. Brains always interact with other brains. Potentials therefore unfold through meaningful interactions of preferably different people [1]. The more different people are, the more abundant the possibilities. People cannot not interact. They have no choice. They must cooperate. But they don't always want to. Preferably they ought to cooperate with different people. But this they like even less. At this point tensions, contradictions and sensitivities arise.

Here you can create an influential impact now. I know you want it. I know you think it's difficult. And it is. It is very challenging.

But it is possible.

Content

Part 1
The Contradictory Inner Life of People

Have you ever met someone like Harold? Harold is always on the move, knows everything and is always willing to help. He has been working as a laboratory technician for many years, but without any leadership responsibility. But he constantly offered his boss to do all kinds of things for him. He is also very enthusiastic about getting his colleagues on their toes. The boss refused, of course. Initially. But then the day came when he became weak. Harold is really helpful, and he gets things done. He acts where others just talk. From that day on Harold had his foot in the door and his boss could no longer say no when he forced his help on him. Since Harold is not fully occupied, he and his wife have started a small catering service. There is hardly a department in the company where he has not already organized a birthday party or buffet. He's doing really well. He is really fast, useful and inexpensive. No one gets past him. He is always there and waiting for his opportunities. The downside, however, is that some colleagues are quite annoyed by him. Would you want to connect with Harold?

Many hesitate at this thought. That's understandable. Living together with people is not always easy. People have three qualities that will constantly challenge you:

- People are contradictory.
- They are over-sensitive.
- At the same time, they are equipped with most awesome capabilities.

However, the enriching moments that await you are worth every effort.

Suppose you have chosen Harold and want to integrate him into your life. In the beginning you will have the feeling that Harold is a great enrichment. He actually behaves as described above. He looks for ways to help you, takes work off your hands, cannot sit still and is constantly active. After a while he knows all your friends and acquaintances and takes care of your social network. He makes appointments for you, organizes your free time, decides with whom and when you meet. He also participates helpfully in your leisure activities at any time. Your friends and acquaintances take him to their hearts and soon he will be a part of your small community. This community is growing and new acquaintances are being made. Suddenly you realize that Harold has changed your life. You take a moment, think about it and realize the following: You have not integrated Harold into your life, but Harold has integrated you into his life. It was not you who took responsibility for Harold, Harold took responsibility for you. You are not leading Harold. Harold is leading you. Harold has taken over your life. Capture through helpfulness.

Now ask yourself: Is this good or not? Do I want this or not? You realize that this question is not easy to answer, because Harold is a great guy. You do not want to disappoint him, you do not want to curb his enthusiasm, you want to provide him with a joining-forces-appropriate habitat. At the same time, you think it is necessary to talk to him about living together. You feel the need to discuss roles and responsibilities and to sort it out somewhat differently. You invite him for a conversation:

You:	»Harold, we need to talk.«
Harold:	[Startled] »Yes, what?«
You:	»I think we have to sort out our living together in some way.«
Harold:	»What do you mean? Did I do something wrong?«
You:	»No, of course not.«
Harold:	»Well then, that's fine. By the way, I have a great idea for next weekend. You always wanted to go with Giselle and Toby up to the peak of the Little Cow Horn in the Black Mountains with this new cable car. I already got you tickets and I made reservations for a table in the restaurant for you.«

Now Harold looks at you full of anticipation. What are you going to say now? We will now look into this question in detail.

- What do you perceive in people?
- How do you sort and classify what you see?
- What can you do then?

Before you make a decision whether or not and with who you want to live together, it is helpful to understand what is going on inside a human being. Yes, humans have an »inside«, an inner life. From the outside we cannot always see it immediately, but this is the key to successful coexistence. Whoever can perceive and sort the signals of the inner life of another person can also arrange living together in a way that is beneficial for all.

Observing, seeing, sorting and understanding are therefore the preliminary steps of all decision-making processes. This is not easy, however. Often it is even difficult for the individual person to understand himself. Man is often a mystery to himself. But if this first step already seems to be a serious hurdle, how challenging will it become to proceed and make the right decision?

There are people in very diverse forms and everyone behaves somewhat differently. These differences make the choice complicated. Don't look at the outside first. The exterior is secondary for a successful living together. Pay attention to the inside of the other one first. To do this you must know your own inner self. Then you can relate this to the inside of the other. Then it becomes possible to predict whether you will live together harmoniously with the person of your choice.

In most cases, the key to this is *similarity*. This applies in any case to the initial phase of the relationship. With this we get to know a first characteristic of the inner life of people: The desire for similarity.

01
Similarity – Blessing and Curse

The overall development process of humans is subject to evolution, as it is with all living beings. People are natural produces. Evolution promotes traits and characteristics that ensure long-term survival. It does not have the survival of a single human being in mind, but the survival of the entire species. For the individual human being this frame of mind is too large. He sees himself primarily as an individual and cares for himself first. You too would like your human companion to feel comfortable as an individual in his or her own life span and perhaps even to develop a little further. In order for this to succeed, it is helpful to take a brief look at the larger evolutionary picture.

In order to survive on this planet as a species, humans need a multitude of different abilities. One person alone does not have all these. Thus, nature has developed a division of labor. Everyone has different abilities in different forms. Note: Everyone (!) has abilities and everyone is a little different. On one hand, this is good because it means that all people together have all the necessary skills. On the other hand, there is the challenge of bringing these differences together in a meaningful way. This requires a very high degree of overview and coordination. An individual cannot achieve this. This in turn requires joint and coordinated action by many people. At this point we recognize a tricky dilemma. Overview and coordination of different capabilities are best achieved by acting together. An individual cannot manage this alone because he lacks an overall view and merely focuses on his individual interests. How can people then even succeed in achieving meaningful joint action? Here we encounter the first contradiction.

Humans are required to cooperate with each other in order to survive as species. But they are focused on being successful as individuals. They are not prepared to cooperate.

You may expect now that people look for other conspecifics that are completely different. This would be the only way to bring together different characteristics and abilities. But evolution has not developed this as the following example shows.

There are people who like to surround themselves with conspecifics. They always want to be near them. Sometimes it goes so far that they literally stick to each other. Being alone is hard for these people. At the same time, there are people who need more space for themselves, want to be alone and spread out without having to constantly look after another person. Both are fine. Nature has produced both. Both belong to the differences that are important for survival. Now when these two different people meet, the following happens inside of them. Both immediately recognize the differences and THINK: He is different from me and that is actually interesting and good. At the same time, they both FEEL: But the other one is really too exhausting for me and I don't want to get involved in that for the time being.

There is therefore no connection. That which would make life easier and more successful for all people together is often perceived as uncomfortable and disturbing by the individual. What he finds pleasant and desirable, on the other hand, is similarity.

Most people feel sympathetic to other people when they feel that they are like themselves. But if people mainly like people who are similar, then only similar qualities and abilities are combined. Diversity, which is essential for survival is thus restricted and cannot fully develop.

This is another astonishing contradiction.

Potentials unfold through diversity. But people tend to look for their own similar kind.

What nature had in mind is still a mystery. In order to materialize their desire for connection and unfoldment of inherent potentials, people therefore need similarity as a bridge to diversity. This is not a question of external similarities, such as size, weight, appearance, clothing or the preferred car brand, but of internal ones. According to which characteristics are similarities and differences sorted? People actually have distinct inner strategies here. Very fine instincts are at work. In order to be able to sort relevant characteristics of conspecifics, humans must first of all perceive them. And they are capable of doing that. Often unconsciously. Humans are very finely constructed creatures. The first glance at the exterior is sometimes deceptive. This insight leads to the next obvious thought. People are also very sensitive with this inner subtlety. There is hardly a species that gets sick faster, especially internally and emotionally. If you are already considering to maybe refrain from acquiring a human, then this would be completely understandable. This is a responsible and very complex task. Nevertheless, it is advisable to learn a bit more about the secret inner life of a human before you make a final decision. Experience has shown that living together with humans can provide some very happy moments.

02
Six Strengths for One World

The fine perception of people is like a high-resolution radar [2]. When you meet a person for the first time, they will scan you very carefully and meticulously, like at the airport when you go through a body scanner. The scanner better not find anything that irritates or disturbs it. Then it immediately sends a warning signal, but not loudly, rather in complete silence, not perceptible to outsiders. Man does it the same way. He would not utter and address what he perceives aloud, but would turn away from you inconspicuously. This would mean that living together would be under an unhappy star from the beginning on.

How does this mysterious radar work? What is it searching for? When does it send warning signals? This radar is a brain function. Neuroscientists assume that the human brain has not evolved for an estimated 150,000 years because there is no evolutionary pressure [3]. The radar of humans accordingly is an ancient version. But that does not mean that it is useless. On the contrary. We can assume that man is equipped by nature with everything he needs for his survival and development. Nature therefore adds nothing new. Man must do everything else himself. The challenge is to overcome one's own inner contradictions, to activate a fine feeling for the realization of one's special abilities and to network with other people. Then he becomes who he could be.

People have six outstanding abilities, which are in fine balance with each other. Sensitivity is already one of these abilities. First of all, people are resilient and elastic. They can bear a lot. They are also sensitive and empathic. They can record and process the finest signals. This enables empathy. Empathy means that the respective person is able to perceive others very precisely and at the same time reflect on himself at any time. This fine perceptual sensor enables him to transfer his experiences and lessons learned to other contexts. With this transfer ability he can translate inner processes into outer action and from the outer action he can gain material for his inner processes. This extends his radius of perception, makes him mobile and creative. He can think possible options for action into the future and recognize and assess their consequences before they even take place. Transferability and anticipation are the core of human intelligence. Everything experienced and learned unfolds only when it is transferred to concrete life situations and realized in action.

An idea only becomes an innovation when it manifests itself externally with benefits for others.

These two mental steps are very demanding and at the same time the key to human success. They allow an almost limitless space for creative action, especially for joint action.

At a glance. The six special abilities of humans are:

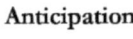

Cooperation

Anticipation

Elasticity
and Resilience

Transferability

Sensitivity
and Empathy

Self-Reflection

Joining forces means giving space to these abilities, developing them and using them jointly in a meaningful way. These skills are interlinked. Without elasticity and resilience there is no sensitivity and empathy, without empathy there is no self-reflection, and without a well-functioning self-reflection at the end of this chain cooperation will not succeed. We already suspect, that, due to the sensitivity of humans, minor disturbances are sufficient to upset this fine linkage of abilities. Resilience becomes the constituent factor for the development of people. Giving them a feeling of security and stability opens up this space for growth. We must therefore treat the human species with care and protect them. That is why we begin our journey into the human interior with a look at their most sensitive instrument, the often-unknown perceptual radar.

03
The Ultra-Fine Inner Radar

The diversity of human abilities begins with sensitivity and empathy. They are responsible for the sensitive radar. Surprisingly, people are often not aware of this fine instrument. Even unconsciously it fulfils its full function. In this case, however, the intercepted signals are not consciously processed, sorted and classified. They generate rather diffuse but nevertheless effective emotional impulses to move towards people or to distance oneself. Under the effect of disconnection, self-reflection and transferability do not develop to their full capacity. Thus, stable and purposeful behavior is only possible to a limited extent. Nevertheless, this radar effectively decides on the next steps a person takes. Let us think back once again to Harold in his professional environment. His colleagues receive multiple and therefore ambiguous signals, cannot consciously classify them and are consequently confused. The confusion leads to feelings of disturbance. The colleagues are annoyed. This could result in conflicts. This could be avoided. Harold is, as we will see later, a completely normal person. He only has an unusually large number of interests and talents, which he rather uses without focus. Whoever knows this and can sort and understand these behaviors gives Harold a safe and structured space. There he will be able to use his skills for the benefit of others. Awareness of these inner processes avoids conflicts and promotes joint action.

There are probably three main reasons for the development of the radar: Recognizing danger - hunting - partner selection. People are easily frightened. Fear of hunger, need and all kinds of dangers. In the end they are afraid of death. In order to protect themselves from this, people began early on to organize themselves into groups. Probably similarity of needs and habitat for this was the binder. At the same time, a feeling of difference and individuality compared to other groups developed, up to a feeling of competition, antagonism and enmity. Between groups of people the same principle applies as between individuals. Here too, joint action ensures survival. And here too, the need for similarity stands in the way of joint action with others. This results in a new source of danger: other people. People are afraid of people [1 - page 103]. This sounds strange, contradictory and rather nonsensical, but at the same time it is reality. The fact is, humans are very sensitive and therefore very vulnerable. The radar is therefore used to a large extent to assess inconveniences or dangers at an early stage, including those caused by people. At the same time, humans learned early on that they need cooperation partners in order to survive successfully, for example when hunting together. This has brought forth another ability in him. He is very observant. Are you familiar with this situation? You are standing at a bus stop, waiting and have the strange feeling that someone is watching you. What do you feel then? Are you happy about it? No, probably not. Those who feel »watched« notice this very quickly. They get nervous after about 10 seconds. The brain signals: Someone's watching me. The instinctive feeling of becoming prey of a hunt arises. If this condition continues a little longer, the human body will develop an increasingly strong defense reaction. So, avoid watching people for too long. They could then become restless and unfriendly.

In addition to danger assessment and hunting, humans naturally also need the radar for partner selection. Deep down he looks for connections with other people that are safe, meaningful, reliable and profitable. Details are important and therefore his radar is also very finely tuned. There is an infinite number of signals that have an effect on people. The natural radar filters out the most important signals and sorts them in order of importance. This order varies according to the type of person and situation. Twelve criteria are in the foreground.

01. Is the other person a danger to me or is he peaceful?
02. Is the other one present? Is he »with me« or is he focused on himself only?
03. Does he notice me? Will I be seen or does he only see himself?
04. Is he interested in me as a person or does he see me only in my function or usefulness?
05. Does he meet me with appreciation and respect or does he behave in a pejorative and disrespectful manner?
06. Can I easily assess him or does he behave ambiguous and unclear?
07. Is he like me? Are we similar?
08. Is he competent? Is he able? Is he useful for me?
09. Does he »shine« for what he does or does he do this just because he has to?
10. Is he willing to use his skills for my purposes? Does he judge my interests as at least as important as his own or does he represent my interests maybe even with a higher priority (»First serve, then earn«)?

11. Can I rely on him permanently or do I have to fear that he will break his promises?
12. Does he remain stable and reliable even under pressure and adversity?

Only when ALL of these criteria are fulfilled does a person feel safe and comfortable and begins to build trust. If one of these criteria is not met, he is irritated and his scan reacts with a warning signal. The scan then continues with particular intensity. This costs energy and creates feelings of disruption that hinder trust-building and stable relationships. Trust is the prerequisite for lasting and binding joint action. This term is often used inaccurately and misunderstood as an emotional »soft factor«. Behind this is the logical structure of the inner radar with its precise criteria and situation-specific filter strategies. If the signals are unclear, this radar runs almost non-stop. A radar in continuous use costs energy and the brain finds this extremely unpleasant. If instead someone passes the radar positively, the brain can relax, reduce energy consumption to a low-power mode and begin to feel comfortable. People then often say that the »chemistry« is right or they are on the same »wavelength« and that now they can be truly themselves. They associate this state with the feeling and the term »trust«. Now joint action is possible without reservation.

At this point, please ask yourself:

01. Am I friendly and are others safe with me?
02. Am I present when interacting with others?
03. Do I see others or am I mostly focused on myself?
04. Can I discover interesting aspects in others?

05. Am I appreciative and respectful?
06. Am I easily »readable« for others?
07. Can I create a mutual feeling of similarity with others?
08. Do I have anything meaningful to give? Do I contribute in a way which is useful for others?
09. Do I »shine« for what I do?
10. Do I put the other's benefits into the foreground of my action [»First you, then me«]
11. Am I constantly reliable?
12. Do I remain stable under stress, stay connected and being capable of acting?

In general people enjoy all these abilities. At the slightest uncertainty, however, they quickly get out of step and then send contrary signals. Then the trust breaks or it doesn't build up at all. The radar is like a sensitive feeler. It gropes its way forward carefully. At the slightest resistance it flinches. Here we recognize another contradiction that makes living and cooperating together more difficult.

People look for trusting relationships. At the same time, they do not fully trust in advance. The other feels this and withdraws. If he withdraws, the other one withdraws also. A vicious circle unfolds. One of them has to keep his feelers on. Even if the other one twitches. Someone has to take the first step and not give up immediately in case of failure. But who?

Trust is the prerequisite for joining forces. Setting it up is an extremely sensitive and easily disturbed process. Without trust, however, there can be no joint action. Again, we find ourselves in the well-known dilemma. That is why the attempt to join forces requires your full commitment and the utmost attention. Above all, it requires the confident handling of the amazing sensitivity and strange contradictions of people.

04
The Strange Self-Centeredness

If we take another look at the structure of the radar, three elements stand out:

- Am I seen by the other?
- Is it easy for me to »read« the other?
- Are we similar?

Here we recognize another contradictory subtlety. People want to be *seen* [4]. That makes them happy. But they do not want to be *watched*. It makes them nervous. What's the difference? A person who watches and observes another person remains - to use the language of the hunter - under cover. He's keeping a low profile. He does not reveal himself. He's evading the other guy's radar. The latter then cannot assess it and has no possibility of orientation. This leads to uncertainty and resistance. Watching is thus not an act of empathy and cooperation, but an act of demarcation, self-protection and possibly even prey behavior. Scientists say that one turns the other into an »object«. This is clearly an unfavorable signal if we want to win people's trust. A more effective signal is: I see you. Even more effective signals are:

- I see you
- I am also visible for you
- We are similar

This sounds good, but it is not so easy to put into practice. The question is, how can we succeed in overcoming this contradiction?

People want to be seen. But if you want to be seen yourself, you cannot see the other person at the same time. In the end, no one is seen.

When a person wants to be seen, his attention is focused on himself. But then he can no longer pay full attention to his counterpart and give him the feeling of being seen. »I see you« means being completely with the other person at this particular moment. One's own need to be seen is therefore put aside for a second. This is exactly what people find difficult. However, if a person's attention is not completely focused on the conversation partner, it will be immediately detected by the other person's radar. It recognizes that the first person is focused on himself, thus sending a warning signal. This leads to a retreat of the counterpart and not to a movement in the towards direction. This is a dilemma: the desire to be seen is at the same time an obstacle to the fulfilment of this desire. Is this a weaving flaw of nature or is there a secret meaning behind it?

The person now stands at a fork in the road and must make a decision. Does he pay attention to his counterpart or does he want to be in the center of attention himself? In such moments the genius of nature is revealed. A field of tension is created from which humans cannot escape. He cannot not decide. Whether he acts or not, he changes the situation and the interaction with his counterpart. Standing still is impossible. In this seemingly contradictory dynamic, an inevitable tension comes to light, which constantly drives the development of human beings. Having to make decisions thus becomes a building block of evolution. Tensions arising from contradictions are a fundamental prerequisite for human development. Nature grants a glimpse into her finest construction plans.

If people are not aware of the significance of these forks in the road, they make decisions that oscillate diffusely between ego-focus and altruism. The results and impacts are not clear, straightforward and reliable, but confusing and not helpful in building trust. Conscious decision-making, on the other hand, is an evolutionary advantage. This is where man takes the fundamental step towards meaningful and cooperative self-organization.

Do I serve myself or do I serve the other first? You may say now: By serving the other person first, in the end I will serve myself as well. That's smart, and you're absolutely right. But for many human beings this is a dilemma and they often hesitate at this point. Why should they? They can only win in the end. In fact, humans are born with this first-you-then-me altruism. Young children help, share and inform without expecting anything in return [5]. But they learn very early on that others take advantage of this primordial altruism. They then feel hurt inside and feel like losers. Then they take cover, switch their small radar to very large and wait. They maintain this caution even as adults. Herein lies the cause of hesitation and cautious behavior. This impacts interactions with other people in a not so desirable way: The other perceives the hesitation with his fine radar and reacts to it. Very few people respond with an invitation to get to know each other better. On the contrary, they tend to react also with hesitation, retreat or even dominance and set the course for self-focus at this fork in the road. So the opportunity is lost. The more often a person undergoes such experiences, the less willing he is to overcome his learned cautious behavior and take the first step.

This can be well illustrated with an example from German road traffic. Imagine an intersection where no special yield-rule applies. In Germany then the rule is: right-before-left, which means the car from the right has the right of way. Imagine vehicles coming from every direction stopping at the intersection at the same time. All have the same starting situation. What next? Who has the right of way?

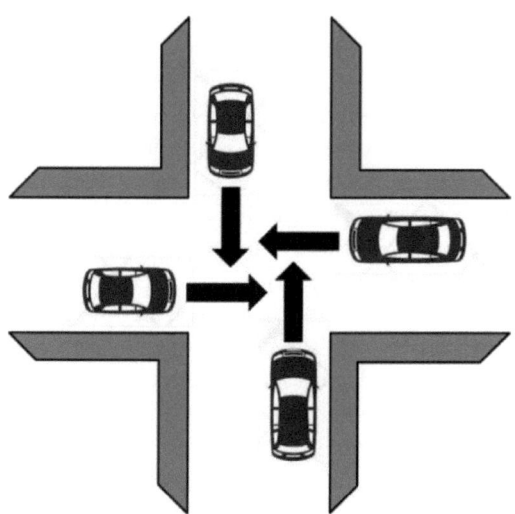

First of all, a rather surprising finding: This case is not regulated by German legislation. Thus, there is a need for self-organization. Someone has to make the first move. Suppose the driver of the lower vehicle does this. He waves to the driver of the left vehicle and allows him the right of way. Then the opposite vehicle follows, then the one on the right. And finally, the one at the bottom. Experience teaches that whoever waves first, drives last.

This is a dilemma and always creates tension. Consciously reflecting and acting people can withstand this tension and overcome the dilemma [6]. »Normal« people tend not to wave, but wait for someone else to wave first. But why would anyone do that? In the end it is not the wiser one who will give in, but very likely the one who is the most unnerved. The latter then also feels like a loser. The result is a spiral of non-yielding. This is how the concept of winning or losing, asserting or giving in is created in the first place. In the end self-centeredness wins. However, this stands in the way of sustainable cooperation.

The contradictions we have considered so far are like right-before-left cross roads. They are forks in the road where people have to make decisions. They cannot escape. They do have choices, though. At the same time, they cannot not choose. In order to be able to withstand this field of tension and make consciously reflected decisions, people need a clear perception of the situation and relevant criteria. But many people do not have this clarity. The following example illustrates this.

A woman goes shopping in a delicatessen. Her husband asked her to bring a bottle of limoncello. She comes home without limoncello.

Man:	»So, what about the limoncello? Didn't they have any?«
Woman:	»Well, yes, lots of.«
Man:	»So, what?«
Woman:	»I was standing in front of the shelf. There were six different varieties, different bottles, colors and origin. And different prices, of course.«
Man:	»So? What's the problem?«
Woman:	»I had to decide«.
Man:	»Yeah, that's what you normally don't have trouble with.«
Woman:	»But I need criteria for that. Form, color, origin and price are no relevant criteria. The only decisive criteria is the taste. And they didn't offer a tasting.«
Man:	»And that's why you didn't buy any?«
Woman:	»Right.«
Man:	»You could have bought just any of these, it doesn't really matter.«
Woman:	»But it's like wine. You don't do that there, do you?«
Man:	»That's different.«
Woman:	»What's different about that?«
Man:	»With wine there are some fine differences. Limoncello always tastes the same, more or less.«
Woman:	»I think we have different points of view.«
Man:	»Next time, just bring any.«
Woman:	»Next time, you can go yourself and get one.«

Who's right? Both of them, of course. What went wrong? They did not agree on relevant decision-making criteria. Both had different criteria. The woman is right, because the taste is probably the only relevant criteria for deli food. The man is right because he too has criteria. No one can decide without criteria. But they were not recognizable to his wife. Nor for us, by the way – probably the degree of alcohol. But we cannot know this because his decision-making process was diffuse. If people at such a fork in the road do not have clear criteria that are appropriate to the situation, they should not make a decision. They should first search for relevant criteria or, if they don't find any, they should go with the second best. Those who don't find any, make diffuse decisions. At these forks in the road, however, there is no option not to choose. Doing nothing is also a decision and triggers further interaction dynamics with other people involved. Diffuse decision making then leads to diffuse interactions and unpredictable reactions. Awareness of the importance of the situation and clear, relevant decision-making criteria are therefore important. People who are not aware of this often make decisions based on self-referential criteria. Remember the scan:

- Does he notice me? Will I be seen or does he only see himself?
- Is he competent? Can he do something useful for me?
- Will he use his skills for me too? Does he put my interests first?

So, if you intend to build trusting relationships with people, then show them that it is worthwhile and above all safe to grant the other person the first sight and offer them the right of way. In the end both will win. You as the one who actively promotes joining forces with a person should ideally start with this and consistently maintain this behavior.

The one who waves first, takes the lead.

If the other person reacts positively, then confirm it and above all do not let him or her look like a loser. In this way, he develops the ability to recognize forks in the road and to make meaningful decisions there. He won't be able to do it alone so quickly. He needs your support for this.

You can help him to sharpen his perception and to kindle cooperation-oriented self-reflection. In the end it is about seeing others, becoming visible and connecting with others through similarities.

What exactly does that mean? What does »seeing« and »similarity« refer to?

05
Five Fundamental Inner Dynamics

»Seeing« and »similarity« refer to the inner identity-forming personality structures of all human beings. On closer look we recognize five clearly distinguishable personality dynamics [7]. We try not to pigeonhole people. They don't like that at all. People believe that they are unique and unmistakable. On a deeper individual level this is definitely true. At the same time, in the course of its long history of development, man has taken on a form that enables quick perception and classification among each other. An example from nature: trees. If you step very close to a group of oaks, you will notice that each oak is unique. This is not surprising, of course. If you take a few steps back and keep some distance, you will notice that all oaks have something in common, something that distinguishes them from other trees. Oaks and birches can therefore be immediately distinguished from each other, because all oaks and birches look the same at the species level, although they are unique at the individual level. In a figurative sense this also applies to the inner structure of people. Similarities and differences relevant for cooperation can be quickly perceived and classified. This is an evolutionary advantage and the subject of the following.

There are five fundamental inner identity-forming personality structures. Here is an overview in the order of prevalence with some descriptive characteristics:

Relationship
Being connected, empathy, belonging, equality, justice, helpfulness

Order
Thinking, criteria, structures, arguments, logic, knowledge, experience, reserve

Achievement
Goals, action, results, clarity, directness, tempo and speed

Territory
Expansion, influence, dominance, power, significance, leadership

Innovation
Freedom, new, uniqueness, inventiveness, ideation, change

Let us take a closer look at this typology. People carry all these personality traits within themselves. Hardly anyone has all five equally pronounced. Each one has its own individual characteristics. Sometimes a single trait is particularly pronounced, and most often there are combinations. Most common are combinations of two with a primary and a secondary preference. Nature has arranged this very cleverly. If people have all these personality traits within themselves, they can also find points of contact and cooperate with everyone else. But for this they do not need all traits to the same degree.

No human being is complete and at the same time every human being is right as he is. People only achieve completeness together.

Someone whose traits would all be equally strong would be surprised and confused about himself. The contradictory nature of these parts would constantly search for balance in his inner being, but would not find it and would hardly ever come to rest. He would like to connect with other people and spend time with them, at the same time he would also have the urge to achieve something and to do it as quickly as possible. At his fast pace, he would lose others in the process, which would make his relationship part suffer. But he doesn't want to be stopped either. At the same time, it would be important for him to think things through carefully, in as much detail as possible, undisturbed by others, therefore acting with reserve. His preference would be to secure tried and tested procedures and avoid unnecessary change. Again, at the same time, he would have new ideas every day and would have no desire at all to do repetitive work. Moreover, he would like to expand and go for the big picture, not necessarily wanting to take into account the slow and the hesitant.

This personality would not only be confusing for others, but also for himself. All those contradictions would merge. It would be difficult for this person to establish his or her own inner order and to connect permanently with others. Therefore, such a personality structure is rare. Nature is graceful.

However, there are a few people whose structure comes close to this, i.e. four traits are more pronounced, the fifth trait is less effective. Linda is a good example of this. She has a strong territorial trait linked to relationship, achievement and innovation. On the other hand, the degree of order is not so pronounced. Imagine such a person. She enjoys strong self-confidence and a very present appearance, sometimes direct, slightly uninhibited and at the same time with great warmth of empathy. No one can escape such a strong, warm and convincing »hug«. In addition, there is an innovative, game changing abundance of ideas, which is guided by the desire to act energetically and to create something big and meaningful. Fascinating and charismatic. Unique. A classic high-level networker.

On this occasion we can also solve the mystery of the term »charisma«. As charismatic, we experience people who have opposing personality traits, who have successfully integrated them with each other and can thus draw from a variety of behavioral patterns. The presence of such people triggers a special resonance in us. Our radar starts to oscillate and senses this effective combination of different personality components. For a moment, the perceived contradictions are overcome. In this consonance the own different traits are connected. An unknown synergy becomes noticeable. An own inner cooperation between the different parts of our personality takes place, the own inner parts meet and connect. Unknown potentials become energized. A deeper human experience unfolds and is fulfilled. Something he longs for and yet rarely experiences. This experience of resonance leads to the feeling of charisma. If this charismatic person is also free and independent, sees us as a person and wants to share something joyful with us, material or immaterial, then we are at the feet of this person. With artists this happens frequently. As said, fascinating and unique. Sometimes there are also sales people with such a personality structure. Then please hold on to your wallet.

Let us now turn to »normal« cases. The most common personality traits are RELATIONSHIP and ORDER in many different forms and combinations. Let's start with the relationship part.

Relationship
Being connected, empathy, belonging, equality, justice, helpfulness

People with a strong relationship part value connectedness and involvement in trusting and harmonious relationships. If the atmosphere among themselves is good, they can make good and valuable contributions. Justice is highly important for them. It means that everyone is treated in the same way, or everyone gets equal shares. Here is a scene that actually happened. In a team of four people there was a very strongly relationship-oriented man. After lunch he came back to the office with a candy bar. With »one« candy bar. Then he unpacked it, divided it accurately into four equal parts and distributed them to his colleagues and himself.

Such people are usually very compassionate, can judge others well and establish trusting relationships. This is the basis of self-esteem of a relationship-oriented personality. Empathy and a good sense and feeling for the other person have a positive effect on others. The feeling of being seen and perceived arises and this strengthens their self-value. Such people take time for others, like to listen, share and help.

These people have a special **trust strategy**. They give others trust in advance, unless the trust has previously been abused. Then they hold back. But in principle they are prepared to meet new acquaintances with a trusting attitude. This must be taken into account and must be treated with care. Maybe now you're thinking: If all people were like that, then cooperation would work out perfectly. You're right about that. But be careful. Every personality trait has two sides. Cooperation also means that all - even different - points of view are exchanged and processed and are ultimately included in the following decision-making and implementation. There are always majorities and minorities. Supposed winners and supposed losers. This hurts relationship-oriented personalities. At this point they hesitate. The fear arises of dominating and hurting other people and thus straining the relationship. Compromises could now be reached which do not do justice to the matter and lead to a loss of quality. In hesitation lies the risk to create a decision-making vacuum. Especially territorial, achievement- and order-oriented people would sense this vacuum and instinctively fill it. They would intervene in the decision-making process, take it over and impatiently or dominantly take the lead. In such a situation the relation person would have to defend his territory. This is difficult for him, however, because he would have to separate and distance himself from the »opponents«. A very unpleasant situation. His desire for harmonious connectedness would contradict this. Of course, this does not mean that relationship people cannot stand their ground. It's just not that easy and comfortable for them. It does not correspond to their authenticity. To display such behavior is rather stressful for them. They then often say that they do not want to bend or become another persona. But this has nothing to do with bending, because such people also have a territorial trait, even if it's small. It just feels uncomfortable to activate this part because it is the opposite of the familiar authentic part. We call this inner authentic area of experience and action the »comfort zone«. We understand this in a positive sense. It is often used disrespectfully for people who do not want to change and prefer to stick to habits. What is meant here, however, is the individual and authentic state of a person. There he has the optimal access to his energy, abilities and potentials. From there he can connect with others and work successfully.

In this sense, the comfort zone is a person's »power room«.

Let us assume a relationship person works as an insurance salesman. He then will be able to quickly build up trust with potential customers. At the end of such a sales talk everyone feels comfortable. Now, however, the salesperson has to do something which, for him as a relationship person, is connected with the fear that it could destroy the well-established relationship. He must bring the sales pitch to a closing. He must ask the customer to make a decision. He has to ask the so-called closing question:

»We have now discussed and clarified all issues. We can put this contract into effect now. Are you ready to sign it?«

There is only a yes or no to this question. Of course, the salesperson knows this and might be afraid of it. A »No« often is experienced by a relationship person as rejection of his person and thus as rejection of the offer to connect. Of course, we all know that this is not meant that way and that a salesperson does not have to take a »No« personal. But KNOWING and FEELING are two different categories. Even if he or she knows that the »No« only refers to the factual level, a relationship person cannot prevent it from feeling like an unpleasant personal rejection. There are many relationship-oriented people in interactive decision-making functions. That's perfectly all right, too. The personality structure says nothing about the respective qualification. It only says something about the well understood comfort zone and its limits.

So, you see, there are two sides to every personality trait. Some may now think of a good and a bad side, or a light and a dark side. This would not be appropriate and would not do justice to the fine quality of these personality traits. If one thinks in good and bad or light and dark, then very easily unjustified devaluations take place.

Caution: Devaluations

Devaluations often arise from not well reflected and misunderstood perceptions of differences. So, what could the other personality types think about our relationship person?

An order person may think: He is too emotional, too non-factual, too influenced by feelings instead of arguments, addicted to harmony and afraid of conflict.

An achiever thinks: He is too slow, too less goal-oriented, more interested in coffee parties, too considerate, not flexible enough.

A territorial or power person may think: He is not equal, cannot hold his stand, not cut out of the same block, a weakling.

The innovator thinks: He is far too cautious, too concerned with safeguarding, not brave enough, too stuck in his own boundaries, too dependent on others, too unimaginative, uncreative, nice but boring.

All these stereotypical ways of thinking are understandable and at the same time unjustified. They are understandable because they follow the dynamic that people like each other when they experience themselves as similar. Conversely, they tend to keep their distance when they meet people who are different. If this initial and instinctive distance is not quickly overcome, it can lead to disconnection, dissociation and rejection, even to devaluation and enmity. They are unjustified because they say nothing about the quality of the other person, only about his authentic identity dynamics and his fundamental emotional preferences. They are the way they are. And this is beyond judgement. This is where human dignity is rooted. And dignity is the non-touchable core of his being. Furthermore, these stereotypes are self-damaging because we know that it is only in cooperative connection of these different personality parts that people can unfold their potentials.

In this sense people are never complete, but always right.

Considering this, let us not think in good or bad, in strengths or weaknesses, but rather think of a face of a medal and a back of a medal. Like a gold-medal.

The Face of the Medal – Relationship

- Building and maintaining relationships
- Supporting team spirit
- Establishing affiliation and connection
- Empathizing
- Sharing
- Sponsoring
- Balancing
- Building trust
- Making compromises instead of imposing results

The Back of the Medal – Relationship

- Avoiding conflicts
- Dodging adversity
- Harmony comes before assertiveness
- Appeasing instead of acting consequently
- Supporting rather than demanding

Behind this are hidden needs and fears.

Needs: Safety, secureness, love.

Fears: Helplessness, isolation, loneliness, abandonment, being lost.

Scan and Similarity: When you meet a relationship-oriented person now, you know more about how he will scan you. Under the criteria of similarity, he will check whether you are present, approachable, caring, patient, whether you can listen, whether you are interested in him as a person, whether you take the time to get to know him or whether you are only interested in material and selfish benefits. Whether you are willing to share and help and whether you are peaceful and friendly.

This is what an instruction manual for a person with a high relationship trait could look like. But there is a hurdle. Suppose you are an order personality and facts are more important to you than sharing emotional states of mind. You'd rather talk about fact-based topics and relevant details. Following the »manual«, you should now take some time, start with talking about personal matters, have a coffee together in peace and only then move on to the more factual levels. An order person understands this, of course, and he could do it, but it does not correspond at all to his comfort zone. In doing so he would feel like bending and compromising himself in order to establish a trusting rapport with the other person. He would feel awkward. At this point, resistance arises. This resistance is turned against consciously creating similarity with people who show clear differences in their personality compared to oneself. However, this resistance stands in the way of successful cooperation. Here again our dilemma becomes visible. Let's take a closer look. You will notice in the following that the language we use in this book adapts to the respective personalities. This serves the purpose to make it easier to read for the person addressed. At the same time, it should give you an impression of how you can establish trust with different personalities using the right language without stretching too much. Language becomes a »tool«, which does the work for you.

Order

Thinking, criteria, structures, arguments, logic, knowledge, experience, distance, reserve

People with a high degree of order-orientation expect procedures to be plausible and logically thought through. This requires structured thinking, which unfolds along relevant criteria. These criteria must derive from facts and knowledge and not - as with the husband in our Limoncello example - from diffuse emotional states. Experience and action should have a rational basis and be largely uninfluenced by emotional feelings. »Objective feelings« based on knowledge and experience are allowed. These people experience structure and order as an inner scaffolding that provides security and serves as the basis for external coherence and inner cohesion. Order people in organizations appreciate hierarchies because they are the prerequisite for construction and development. They also appreciate and preserve the proven achievements of the past until there is enough secure experiential knowledge to break new ground. Fairness is a high value and means that decisions are made on the basis of reasonable arguments and clear criteria. Fairness does not mean equal treatment. Equal treatment is not a criterion in its own right, but rather the consequence of criteria, if all the decision-making factors are indeed equivalent. Which they normally are not. For order people there are endless ways of making distinctions down to very small details. Unequal treatment of inequalities is fair for order people. Correct behavior, reserved politeness and controlled emotionality are further characteristics of them. It is important that others treat them with respect. This includes keeping a certain distance during the first encounter, getting closer to each other appropriately through more factual exchange and not pushing for decisions too early. In public, they don't like crowds, sitting too tightly on planes, trains or busses and above all they disdain obtrusive loud phone calls from self-absorbed busybodies.

If you invite an order person to your home for a dinner with friends and he comes first, it would be a slight mistake to tell him with a happy smile: »The table is all yours. Pick a seat.« This is unpleasant for an order person. He cannot recognize and assess the house rules, does not want to take anyone's traditional place and would feel a little disoriented at the table alone. It wouldn't help him either if you told him now: »By the way, we take it easy, we have no special order here. Feel free.« This would increase the dissimilarity and unnecessarily strain the comfort zone of the order person. Probably his inner scan would now be in a state of alarm and he would ask himself: »What am I doing here at all and how can I get out of this situation as fast as possible?« So, what would be a joining-forces-appropriate behavior on your part as a host? Welcome him, do not leave him alone and offer him a pre-planned seat.

Host:	»Welcome. You are the first guest tonight and I'm really glad.«
Guest:	»Oh dear, I'm the first one?«
Host:	»I'll go ahead and show you where we are going to have dinner tonight. Would you mind following me?«

Guest:	»Pleasure. Thank you.«
Host:	»This is the table. We thought we would reserve this seat for you. Here you have everything in view in the best possible way. Is this all right for you?«
Guest:	»That's very kind of you.«
Host:	»May I start by getting you something to drink?"
Guest:	»I'd love to, but nothing alcoholic, please.«
Host:	»Absolutely. Would you prefer something fruity?«
Guest:	»Thank you very much, gladly. By the way, who did you invite tonight, if I may ask?«
Host:	»Of course. While we wait, I give you an overview ...«

Remember the scan. The guest will register every detail of your behavior and - as in this example - will gratefully recognize that you respect his needs. In this way you honor him as a person and value his self-esteem.

If you are a relationship or achiever person, you will again find that this behavior does not correspond to your comfort zone. However, you can easily solve this dilemma by using suitable language.

Order does not necessarily mean that the desk or the apartment is tidy. Order is rather to be understood as an inner order, which is characterized by logical thought structures and detailed perception. This leads to an interesting phenomenon. This creates an interior space that provides orientation and in which the person can stay and move autonomously. Think of it as an archive with many compartments and drawers, like a library with many books in which knowledge and experience is collected. Order people can access it any time. This has two consequences: First, they have strong internal references and second, they like into retreat into this interior realm. The following three examples show what is meant by internal references.

You go out to dinner with a friend, read the menu, don't know exactly what you want to eat and ask your counterpart: »What are you having today?« Your companion makes a suggestion and you say: »Oh, yeah, I'll take that, too.«

So, for your decision you need an external indication, an impulse or a recommendation. This is an external reference. You also know this from American movie posters. Most Hollywood movies are starred by two or three famous movie actors. This is not necessarily motion picture arts, but rather marketing. And even though these actors are well-known, you will always find a reference to an equally well-known film in which they've played before: George Clooney – Ocean's Eleven. This is also an external reference, doesn't make much sense at first glance, but helps people without distinct internal references to decide faster - not necessarily better. An order person would now say: »Clueless people must be told how to decide«.

Nice is also this well-known scene: Man leaves the house. Wife looks at him and says: »You can't go out into the streets like that.« Man looks down at himself and says: »Why not?« »Hey, don't you see that? The colors don't match and you picked the wrong pair of shoes.« No, the man can't see that because he lacks internal references. So, he needs his wife as a clothing consultant.

This is unlikely to happen to people with a strong order-orientation. They almost always have sufficient experience and relevant criteria to be able to make their own decisions at any time. Internal references are therefore experience- or knowledge-based relevant criteria applicable for different contexts. In this way the autonomous interior of order-oriented personalities develops and shapes itself. They like to retreat into this interior. Here outer and inner realities merge into one another. For order people neither flight nor resignation is associated with this interior space. It is more of a strategic retreat, where they can review and re-sort the facts and arguments, where they can reflect and sort themselves in peace.

Such people do not like the so-called bath in the crowd. They are rather reticent in their external and relationship orientation. Their inner psychological world thus serves their outside-inside balance. Strongly extroverted people are irritated by this. Relationship people then sometimes think that the order person does not like them. But this is usually not the case. Whoever can assess this correctly can deal with order people in an appropriate manner.

Anyone who cannot adequately assess this, could end up in such a scene: A man is invited on a Saturday to a summer party of friends and is supposed to bring his new girlfriend with him. The party will take place in a »garden«. In reality it is a piece of fenced meadow with a wooden shack and bulky second hand furniture. In large cities where green spaces are scarce, this sometimes serves as favorite escapes. The new girlfriend is - as we already feared - a strong order person. In the morning the following dialogue unfolds:

Man:	»Tom invited us to a garden party today. Do you like to join me?«
Woman:	»But I don't know anybody there«.
Man:	»That's why it's a great opportunity. You'll get acquainted with all of them finally.«
Woman:	»But for me these are all strangers. I don't really know.«

That's the way it goes back and forth. Valuable time passes. In the afternoon, the man had convinced or persuaded his girlfriend to come to the garden party. At this time, however, most of the people there are already sweaty and drunk. Man and girlfriend arrive at the garden gate. Big hello. The first one's stagger towards the man and greet him effusively with hugs and kisses. We're just friends. The man is okay with that. Now we come to a fork in the road - appropriate greeting of order people at garden parties. If properly done, the man would introduce the woman to everyone, keep a certain physical distance to the »strangers«, offer her a seat and something to drink and allow her to accommodate in her own pace. We already notice that a garden party with many strangers on a Saturday afternoon is not the most preferable way to get in touch with order people. At this fork in the road, everyone took a wrong turn. The drunk guests meant well, thought »similarity always fits« and staggered towards the new girlfriend as joyfully drunk as they were and welcomed her with hugs and kisses as they had done with their buddy. She made a face like biting into a lemon and was completely shocked. It was predictable. Such people don't like this. Similarity always refers to the target person, not to oneself or, as here, to companions of the target person. That was well meant, but badly presented. Sitting on the old furniture did not make it any better. After only five minutes she asked her boyfriend: »When are we leaving?«

Incidentally, this sometimes happens in male-dominated companies when men want to integrate newly hired women in a particularly well-intentioned and courteous manner [If you, dear female reader, enjoy an order-oriented personality, the term »integrate« may have immediately triggered a clear and understandable sense of disturbance]. They then treat them as if they were men. For example, on Friday afternoon after work, they invite them to the weekly beer binge, drink, smoke, hoot, tell bad jokes and think how great, open and liberal they are - similarity. Unfortunately, this is a severe misunderstanding and not so funny for the women. A large international company held a management meeting at its production site in China. All men. One woman. Everyone liked her. No differences or prejudices. In the evening they ended up in a brothel. With the woman. It was only there that the gentlemen realized that they had probably overlooked a detail.

Order people have a special **trust strategy**. They do not give trust in advance, but rather let the other run through a particularly precise grid. How competent is he? Does he think in logical steps? Is he fact-oriented? Does he keep respectful distance? The other must prove this to the order person. Repeatedly. And it's not enough to deliver results on time, but also show how he achieved those results in detail. Again, repeatedly. Not just once. How often? Nobody can tell. This may take some time. Bring patience and stamina.

The order-oriented person thinks of himself: »If everyone would be like me, then the world would be in order and would function in an optimal way.« That is of course true. At the same time, however, there are not only order people in this world. And here the back of the medal becomes visible. If you send an order person to a network party with hundred strangers and ask him to come back with ten new relevant contacts, this feels like maximum penalty for him. Such people need more time than others to establish rapport and build trust. However, trust is the prerequisite for cooperation. If one needs more time for this than others and if these others are not aware of the fact, then this time requirement is perceived as distance or even as rejection - and cooperation cannot develop. Cooperation is not on the frontline for a person with strong internal references anyway. He constantly asks himself: »Why should I work together with others at all? I know best how to do it. The other guys are just holding me back.« When an order person has command of a big deal of knowledge and experience, this shapes his or her self-esteem and identity. He looks at other people and thinks: »They're all much stupider than me.« That's not even meant in an arrogant way. For an order person this is simply a factual statement. And these are not ideal conditions for cooperation. You can see that the thing with the joining-forces-appropriate togetherness does not become easier. Devaluations are also in the air here.

Caution: Devaluations

What might other personality types think about our order-oriented person?

Relationship: He shows too little emotion, much too objective, too impersonal, closed, not approachable, dry, a loner.

Achievement: He is much too slow, too detail-oriented, too inflexible, bureaucratic, skeptical and a smart aleck.

Territory: He is not equal, too narrow-minded, but quite useful when it comes to numbers.

Innovation: He is too attached to old and narrow thinking habits, risk-averse, »bottleneck«, boring, uninteresting.

Devaluations can be prevented by looking at the good qualities.

The Face of the Medal – Order

- Knowledge and experience
- Criteria-based structured thinking
- Arguments and logic
- Good perception and a sense for details [Experts are people who see or hear details that others cannot perceive].
- Sense of fairness
- Reliability
- Prudence
- Dry humor

The Back of the Medal – Order

- Avoiding to share personal matters
- Restrained emotionality
- Dislike of »tactical« networking

- High detail orientation to the degree to make life of others miserable
- High independence up to withdrawal from interactions
- Aversion to small talk and establishing contact

Needs: Profound knowledge, proven mental coordinates, structure, orientation.

Fears: Disorder, chaos, senselessness, losing orientation, falling into a bottomless pit, losing hold.

Scan and Similarity: When you meet an order person, he or she will check whether you are factual, structured, respectful, polite and correct, whether you are interested in his or her knowledge and experience or only in superficial small talk, whether you take time for respectful acquaintance and whether you yourself have knowledge and experience that you are willing to share, and whether you are even willing to learn from him or her.

Now you have an instruction manual for a person with a high level of order. That's easier said than done again. Suppose you are an achievement-oriented person, you want to get to the point quickly and save time in conversations. Following the manual would mean to prepare for the conversation in a structured way and discuss the details on the basis of an agenda with many sub-items.

An achiever already suspects this and becomes nervous and impatient even before the conversation starts. This is a huge challenge for its comfort zone.

Let's take a closer look then at these interesting personalities. Quick and to the point.

Achievement

Goals, action, results, clarity, directness, tempo and speed

For achievement-oriented people, only results count in the end. They are focused, fast and want to get to the point. Clarity. Speed. Action. Results. No waste of time. They experience other people as slower. Consequently, they are often impatient. They prefer to do tasks themselves before they explain it to others. Takes too much time. They talk faster, move faster and prefer to eat their sandwiches while walking. They can never really stop. If everyone was like that, we'd all be done sooner. It's pretty neat, huh?

»Faster« always refers to others who are different, in this case slower. If everyone was like that, these other slower ones wouldn't exist. Then there'd be no faster one. Then everything would be equally fast. What good would that do? None. The pace would be relative. There wouldn't be any moderation in it. Besides, nobody would then take time for the details, for thorough thinking, for searching and discovering. Something like Gödel's incompleteness theorems would never have been conceived then. That would have taken too long. Too complicated. The Adagio in Beethoven's 3rd Symphony would not last 15 minutes, but at most seven and a half. Anyway, one would be out of the concert hall faster.

Achievement-oriented people are cool, but for our overall goal, cooperation, they would sometimes need to slow down so that others can dock and not be blown away by the airstream. This is difficult for achievers. That's not their comfort zone.

Is cooperation between different people even possible under these conditions? Now somebody might get the idea that the individuals just have to adapt a little. The relationship person would have to become a little more direct, the order person a bit more emotional and the achiever slower. But HOLD! This then is no longer cooperation of different authentic people, but an attempt to level human diversity and make everybody equal and kind of medium sized just to avoid discomfort and challenge. The message would be: »I don't like the way you are. As you are, you're not useful. Become someone other than who you are«. That would be conformity terror. Above all, this would violate people's self-esteem and lead to a very special phenomenon in the human behavioral repertoire: resistance.

Those who are in resistance do not cooperate. We will take a closer look at this particular topic later. Now quickly the **trust strategy** of the achiever. It's quite simple: If the other person quickly gets to work, finds solutions and gets results fast enough and shows the whole thing two or three times, then trust is created.

Actually, simple and cool. Nevertheless, there is danger of devaluation again.

Caution: Devaluations

What could the other personalities think about our achiever?

Relationship: He is too impersonal, too less time for really getting to know each other, only looking for goals and not for togetherness, superficial, hectic, constantly stressed out, actually pitiful.

Order: He is much too superficial, no sense for details, error-prone, not thinking through, too pushy, actually annoying.

Territory: Strange, always on the move, but useful, you can really get him to work.

Innovation: He's like a High-Speed Train in fixed tracks, only forward, and sooner or later he will derail. But he's actually great if he would take time for new ideas.

Devaluations can be prevented by looking at the good qualities.

The Face of the Medal – Achievement

- Quick thinking
- Speed and fast action
- Getting to the point quickly
- Looking for clarity
- Being direct
- Not playing political games
- Competing
- Seeking challenges
- Testing limits
- Delivering results

The Back

- Impatience
- Little willingness to delegate
- Tendency to become workaholic
- Risk of burnout

- No time for furthering relationships
- Not much diplomacy

Needs: Moving, acting, impacting, performing.

Fears: Standstill, powerlessness, uselessness, loss of the right to exist.

Scan and Similarity: If you now meet an achiever, you will know more about how he will scan you: He will check whether you are quick and clear, get to the point and act fast. This is enough to build quick rapport. Then it kicks off. That was fast, well, for achievers. But let's slow down, two things, very briefly:

Danger of Burnout and Exploitation

The pace of achievers is basically an authentic behavioral characteristic. However, no one can say what tempo is authentic and at what tempo the red area starts. Even achievers themselves are sometimes unable to assess this limit. Therefore, there is a danger that they will still put more on their shoulders. Well, it works until it doesn't work anymore. But then it's too late. This behavioral dynamic often arises as a result of compensation needs, especially when achievers come from families where good was never good enough or where the relatives could never develop their potential. This means that the achiever wants to permanently fill a perceived emotional void through performance. Since this emptiness comes from a bygone era and a different environment, the efforts can never lead to real satisfaction. This void cannot be filled afterwards. It always remains. Therefore, these efforts are in vain. Instead of giving up, the achiever almost compulsively continues. More and more. Until burnout.

The solution lies in letting go, stopping and putting an end to it. But this is connected with the feeling of being useless. The inner sentence of many achievers is: »If I achieve a lot, I am allowed to exist and belong.« The human species as such is very sensitive at this point and gets sick quickly. Mostly on the inside. For outsiders this is often not understandable. On the other hand, if you're in it, there's little escape. If you have taken such a person into your close personal sphere, tell him the following and tell him very slowly: »You are allowed to be the way you are.« This gives the achiever a space for peaceful and appropriate being. In addition, you don't take advantage of him. You could have done something else. You might think that this person is driven by an immense urge to perform and I take advantage of that. Achiever are often exploited. As employees in companies they are often promoted because of their performance. But not always for the benefit and development of the person, but often for the self-interest of the decision-makers.

We have just discussed under the headline »Caution: Devaluations« that territorial people in particular consider achievers to be useful. Here the danger of exploitation is particularly great. You can save an achiever from abuse by asking him: »What do you really want for yourself?« He will not always be able to answer this question promptly. Be patient. At some point he will find his own path and gratefully reward you for your patience and dedication.

We have already addressed territorial personalities. Real territorial people have probably already stopped reading this book, if they ever have even started. They do not appreciate that others want to explain the world to them. Understandable. Me too. We have something in common here. If you keep reading, you'll have a benefit for yourself. You learn how to »read« others. You learn how to make good use of others even better. For the big picture, of course. Besides, here comes advertisement for you. So, keep hanging in. All right?

Territory / Power
Expansion, influence, dominance, power, significance, leadership

Territorial or power people are the foremost group of personalities who is often seriously misjudged. Their behavior is perceived as negative, rude, discriminatory or dominant. However, this is not the case. Their behavior is only a special form of normal human dynamics and action.

Such personalities take on tasks or positions like territories. These territories must be conquered, occupied, expanded and above all protected and secured. Courage, determination and assertiveness are therefore among her particularly striking characteristics. They have a true sense for the big picture, for vision and expansion and they are willing to take on responsibility and leadership. This results in a behavioral tendency towards greatness, demarcation and dominance. This is the basis of the self-esteem of power-oriented and territorial people. Others often misunderstand such behavior and have trouble to deal with it properly. For them this behavior looks like an attack. Then they defend themselves immediately or withdraw in avoidance. The power person judges this as weakness and does not take people like that seriously. He seeks and appreciates equal people or even equal opponents. Cut out of the same block. Strong. Unwavering. If they recognize benefits in the other person and if they are steadfast and don't falter easily, then they start to respect them. Then cooperation is possible. Otherwise no chance.

Classic power-oriented people are janitors, groundskeepers, head doctors and party leaders.

The most common misconceptions are:

- Territorial people are rude and impolite.
- They are better leaders.

Territorial people are rude and impolite

Granted, they often behave like that. An example: A new tenant in a high-rise housing estate meets his janitor for the first time and introduces himself politely. If the janitor was a relationship-oriented person, he would now say: »How nice to meet you. Did you have a pleasant move? Have you settled in yet? Are you comfortable in our house? Have you met your neighbors already? Do you need anything?« You have probably already recognized it, relationship-oriented janitors are somehow a rare breed. Our territorial janitor - and this actually happened - reacts like this: He looks at the new tenant from top to bottom and grunts. After a moment he says: »I have fixed office hours and don't call me about every little thing.« Then he turns around and leaves. At first sight this is a bit rough and rude. If we now take a second look at his behavior, a somewhat different picture emerges. What is his inner process? He does what everyone else does. He scans his counterpart mainly for signals of similarity. So, when does someone resemble a power person? What is the power person looking for in the counterpart? What are the key signals?

A power person experiences the others as similar, if they don't behave like weaklings. He recognizes this by the fact that he does not falter under pressure. But in order to recognize this, he must first of all provoke the other one. Here comes the clue: the robust greeting is a test of similarity. Now the power person can read from the reaction of the other one whether he is insecure and confused or stands his ground.

A relational person basically does the same. Just a little different. He may offer a visitor a cup of coffee first and combine this with relationship-oriented words that he lets swing out in a relaxed tone of voice: »Would you like to take a moment and settle in first? May I offer you a cup of coffee?« From the reaction of the other person he can now read whether the other one is a relationship person or not. If the other person becomes slightly nervous before our host has even finished his sentence, he knows that he is an achiever who becomes nervous and impatient at the very thought of »taking a moment to settle in«. No, the achiever wants to get to the point quickly and start the conversation to get over it as fast as possible. The radar then reports: No similarity.

This inner process is the same for all personality types. Only the specific perception filter varies according to type. If you want to pass the radar of a relationship-oriented person, then answer at a slower pace in a type-appropriate manner: »That's nice of you. Thank you very much. I'd love to take a cup of coffee.« A power person would never offer you a cup of coffee like this. He'd say something like: »Coffee's there. Help yourself.«

Now how does our new tenant show the caretaker that he is cut from the same block, does not falter and is in some way similar? In our original case it looked like this. The tenant grunted back and said with a broad gesture: »I see you have a large territory.«

This is a »I-see-you« sentence with a similarity signal. Now something wonderful is happening. Whenever people receive a real »I-see-you« signal, there is a joyful reaction in the brain. The human being feels seen and recognized. The brain then always reacts with a YES. Always. So is our janitor. The Yes was not a clearly articulated Yes, but rather a grunted Yes. But at least a recognizable positive resonance signal. The tenant reinforced this with the following sentence: »And I see you have everything under control.« Now a door opens inside of our janitor and this is - possibly - the beginning of a wonderful friendship.

Important rule at the end: Avoid turf wars with territorial personalities. This incites their self-esteem and when the fight for a territory becomes a fight for honor and self-esteem, then this fight becomes relentless and ends disastrous for all. The appropriate sentence is: »The world is big enough for both of us«. So always keep honor and self-esteem high. This applies to all personality types, of course. Sometimes we overlook this or start conversation in a wrong way. With other personality types than the territorial-power person the consequences are just not as serious.

Why does this misconception even exist? The reason for this lies in the following phenomenon. So far, we have looked at the well-understood comfort zones of the different personalities. When personalities other than the territorial, i.e. relationship, order, achievement and innovation, get into stress and get kicked out of their comfort zone, their relationship dynamic decreases and dominant behavior increases. Even a relationship person then disconnects and starts using his elbows. An order person becomes sharp and precise. An achiever becomes faster and more pushing. Everyone suddenly behaves in a rather rude manner and sets more strict limits. This blurs the boundaries between an authentically territorial person and the other personalities in conflict and under stress. An outside observer can no longer distinguish precisely between comfort zone and conflict zone. In this blurriness the clear view for the territorial personality is lost. His authentic behavior is mistakenly interpreted as stress behavior, which it is not. This is the root cause of wrong judgements.

Power people are better leaders

Territorial or power-oriented personalities definitely like to take the lead. But that does not mean that they are better leaders than others or that someone who seeks leadership necessarily needs to have a strong power trait as primary part of his personality. The personality traits influence the perception-filters of a person and his behavioral preferences. However, they say nothing about the quality of his competences. Type and competences are different categories.

Admittedly, an innovator will hardly want to become an accountant. But he could. An order person will hardly want to become the head of a call center. But he could. A relationship person will hardly want to become the chief of a trade union. But he could. A power person believes about himself, that he could be a good leader. And he could. Like everybody else. There is neither a specific personality type nor a combination of personality components that we can make a positive prognosis for future fulfilment of leadership tasks. Leadership means building relationships and trust, establishing cooperation within teams and towards stakeholders, establishing joint solution and decision-making processes, accompanying a team through its development phases, protecting the team if necessary and finally following through and delivering results. To do so, a good manager needs competences that are related to all parts of the personality. Those who have only one-sided preferences will not be able to achieve this overall, regardless of the basic type. The same applies to a territorial person. Territorial people often prove themselves especially in times of crisis. They then do not discuss endlessly, take the lead, decide quickly. In crisis this behavior is often necessary. But when the crisis is over, power-oriented personalities get stuck in their behavior patterns and are unable to adapt to the new starting position. They sometimes continue acting as if the crisis is still going on. For them there is always crisis. However, this does not allow a team to reorganize itself and find its way back to a common way of thinking, deciding and acting. In the end, this leads to a breakdown of cooperation.

Now you might object that power people are particularly often found in top management positions and that this should probably have something to do with their competencies. Yes, this could be. But there is an additional aspect here, a special interaction dynamic. Power-oriented individuals are in fact often in senior management positions, especially in self-organizing systems such as political parties, churches, trade unions and works councils. In such systems, it is not a professional body that selects the managers, but there is an internal competition for the best positions which is finally solved by elections. This creates a leadership vacuum.

Behavior in Vacuum

In vacuum each personality type behaves differently. A relationship person first looks around, checks how everybody feels and whether someone else might want to take the lead. An order person might say: »How unorganized that everyone is pursuing his own interests now«, and waits and takes the position of an observer. An achiever sets his own goals and begins to communicate them. An innovator offers new ideas to everybody. And the power person? He doesn't talk, he doesn't wait, he just occupies the available room. Right away. Without thinking twice. While the others are still looking around, thinking or developing goals and ideas, he has already taken the space. Clever as he is, he has already created an entourage of allies in advance, which will now strengthen his back. Now the other candidates would have to step more aggressively into the room and claim the role for themselves. Against the power person. That costs extra energy, extra courage and an extra portion of fighting spirit. Relationship people tend to retreat rather than fight. Order people may perhaps make an attempt with the weapon of argument. If they are not heard, they repeat these arguments in other words and perhaps a little louder. If they are then again not heard, they are offended, withdraw and become critical observers. Achievers somehow suffer the same fate. However, they are perceived as useful by the power person and therefore rather pulled into his space of influence and used for his own benefit. Innovators often become court jesters. Power people are often in higher leadership positions not only because they have the greater competence, but also because everyone else has sooner or later avoided the fight and stepped aside. Power people can be good leaders. There is just no automatism.

Do power people also have a **trust strategy**? Of course. They trust people if they are strong and stable, have reliably marked their territories and made safe alliances with them. And if there's the one big thing they can work on together, the better. There may not be many people who have gained the trust of power people, but they do exist.

Some of these comments sound rather critical. It's inevitable. The power person knows that, too. Someone who can expand territorially, who can draw limits and expand boundaries, who appreciates steadfastness, is usually not overly sensitive to other people's feelings and inner processes. This somewhat limited empathy is not a symptom, but a characteristic that constitutes the type. Empathy is necessary for self-reflection. Thus, the self-reflection of a power person turns out to be odd in some way. Every person says of himself that he is right the way he his. In the case of territorial people, they also devalue and sort out those who show avoidance, falter or get scared. This happens with the inner or - sometimes loudly expressed - comment: »If I am too strong, he is too weak. It's his own fault if he can't assert himself.« This makes interaction with others particularly difficult. Cooperation is only possible under special conditions. Divide and conquer. Caesar, Pompey and Crassus. The first Roman triumvirate, 60 B.C. These three men had divided the world among themselves, mistrusting each other at the same time, and for this reason they had established a fine balance of power in which each controlled the other. The political system of the US with its so-called »checks and balances« is an echo of this Roman power orientation and thus an astonishingly current example.

None of this is meant critically. On the contrary it is intended to avoid hasty **devaluations.** So, what could the other personality types think about a territorial or power-oriented person?

Relationship: He is far too dominant, impersonal, cold executioner, dangerous.

Order: He is only interested in himself and his influence, but not in the facts, does not have competence in the details.

Achiever: Acts far too politically, too little interested in clear and focused performance, upper management levels are clubs of old men.

Innovation: He doesn't recognize good ideas, even if you pin them to his office door.

It is advisable not to stick to biases. Then you discover **the Face of the Medal of territorial people,** the shining side of power.

- Being able to see the big picture
- Turning visions into reality
- Tackling challenges
- Making impact
- Facilitating growth
- Providing security
- Delegating
- Creating alliances
- Shouldering responsibility.

The Back,
the somewhat shadowy side of power.

- Marking territories
- Excluding others
- Using pressure
- Testing others for steadfastness
- Applying control
- Political manoeuvring
- Avoiding emotions
- Going for victory or defeat

Needs: Influence, control, domination, Meaning and purpose.

Fears: Loss of control, Insignificance.

Scan and Similarity: From now on, if you meet a territorial person, you will know pretty much how he or she scans you. He will check if you are steadfast, if you are cut from the same block or if you are a weakling.

This sounds plausible, but the question remains for all non-territorial people: how do I create similarity without bending and without getting involved in a turf war? The following picture should illustrate this. Imagine a boxing ring. Inside stands the power person, and you are outside. What happens now? The power person looks at you and thinks: »Well, come on in if you want something.«

STEPPING IN
So, you got to get into the ring. It takes courage, but don't be afraid, nothing has happened yet. Now you stand there. What does the power person think now? He thinks: »Look at this little guy. Well, get closer, if you dare.«

GETTING CLOSE
The power person is first of all surprised and impressed that you have the courage to step into the ring. But don't be too optimistic. You haven't won anything here yet. He's getting curious now. He wants to see how far you get. So, you need to get within range of him, face to face. The tension is rising. You must not wobble, sway, become nervous, defend yourself, take cover or otherwise display insecure behavior. Positively speaking, you simply remain stable and present. Your message is: »This ring is big enough for both of us.«

OUT AGAIN
Figuratively speaking, after this maneuver you better leave the boxing ring again. Your message is: »I am not fighting you. I want to accomplish something. Together with you. Something big. So? Are you in?«

But even now you should not become too optimistic. Even now you have not won anything. What you have won is a ticket into the world of the other. You can look around now. And if you can really contribute something useful and great from the point of view of the power person, you may stay. For a while, at least. Dealing with territorial or power people is not easy. However, if you succeed in gaining access and respect, it is very rewarding. You will then go on a conquest together and leave a footprint in the world. On a grand scale, of course.

Taking the view of the other person – Accompanying the inner processes of the other

We always consider communication and interaction with other people from their point of perspective. Conscious interaction means that we read and understand the inner processes of the other and that we accompany and in some way influence and shape these inner processes.

This is an important step. We overcome our ego-self-focus and try to understand the viewpoints of the other person. We send the signals: »I see you« and »First you, then me«.

Conscious interaction means to explore and understand the inner processes of our counterpart and to accompany them in order to join forces and co-create unfoldment.

Herein lies the secret for type-appropriate interaction with people. »Thinking from the other person's point of view« is a special form of »I see you«. You consciously step back and give space and priority to the other. By this, you pass their scan easily, enable an unconditional encounter, establish a connection and draw a ticket into the world of the other. Now the other one gives you space and priority as well. This is how cooperation unfolds. Our image of the right of way at a right-before-left-intersection takes on a new meaning: whoever waves first creates space for joint interaction and development of potentials.

Carl R. Rogers was probably the first to introduce this type of communication in his famous article »Barriers and Gateways to Communication«, HBR July - August 1952. Nevertheless, this thought has been forgotten again. It is still up to date and almost as new.

»New« is the keyword for innovators, the fifth personality type that we are now turning to.

Innovation
New, freedom, uniqueness, inventiveness,
ideation, change

It is important for innovators to discover the world and experience something new. Changes are not only experienced as opportunities, but as elixir of life. Obstacles are not perceived as challenges, but elementary components of the topography of the living environment of innovation-oriented people. As a result, they do not understand that other people can be evasive or even afraid of change. Innovative people need variety and constant expansion of their thinking boundaries. They are versatile and dazzling. Freedom is a high value for them. This is the main source of their personal motivation and self-value. When looking at situations and assessing them, they see primarily the abundance of possibilities and less the risks. To express and experience uniqueness in thinking, acting and feeling is important for them. Creativity and continuous development are further high values. At the same time, they can give up old things quickly and without hesitation. For this reason, they belong to the class of so-called innovators and early adopters [8]. These are people who are the first to accept and try out innovations in transformation processes.

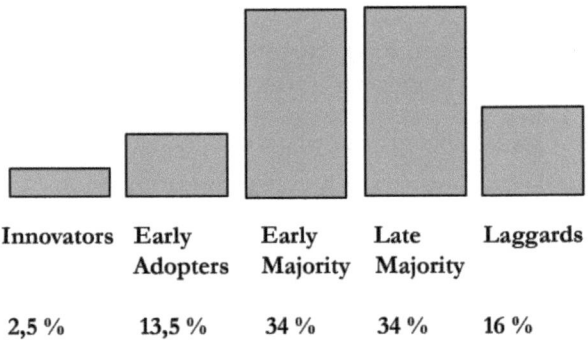

Innovators	Early Adopters	Early Majority	Late Majority	Laggards
2,5 %	13,5 %	34 %	34 %	16 %

People with preferences towards order or relationship, who value deeply rooted and proven procedures, tend to view innovators as frivolous, impermanent, intangible and not very pragmatic. Assigning innovation-oriented engineers the tasks like providing a thorough and detailed documentation at the end of a project could be a difficult undertaking. They will probably have already started working on one or two new projects for quite some time. Maybe even without informing their boss.

Innovators **trust** people who are interesting, which means: similar. Who therefore, bring something new or unique to the table. They also give people who are order- and relationship-oriented trust in advance, because they know that these people are fundamentally reliable and thus stable and trustworthy. However, they find them rather uninteresting and will therefore not make any special efforts. If your goal is to gain the trust of innovators, then show your uniqueness and bring something exciting new with you. In case you don't, at least pay attention to their ideas. Put them in the center. Let yourself be inspired.

Unfortunately, even innovators sometimes experience **devaluations.** So, what could other personality types think about an innovator?

Relationship: He is nice and creative, but very volatile and not real.

Order: He is chaotic, unstructured and, above all, has no respect for the tried and tested.

Achievement: He is interesting, actually cool, but sometimes not realistic enough. After all, something real needs to be accomplished in the end.

Power and territory: Useful now and then, if you manage him properly. Keep an eye on him.

Here again, the same applies: Those who leave these devaluations behind discover

the Face of the Medal – Innovation

- Curious
- Unique
- Visionary
- Pioneering
- Mind boggling
- Creative
- Optimistic
- Versatile

- Inspiring
- Independent
- Free Spirit
- Positive

and the Back

- Unadapted
- Autonomous
- Inaccurate
- Unorganized
- Chaotic
- Nerdy
- Devaluing the tried and tested
- Over-sensitive when facing limitations
- Fighting for freedom constantly

Needs: Freedom to think and act in new and greater spaces.

Fears: Compulsion and limitations.

Scan and Similarities: If you encounter an innovator, you know now how he will scan you and what he is looking for. He will check if you are interesting and inspiring. If you tell him that you enjoy the same holiday destination for 20 years, the conversation will not last very long.

06

Unfoldment of Potentials through Cooperative Diversity

You got a first impression now of the five basic personality structures of people and their inherent motivational dynamics. You therefore hold the key to successful and effective communication and interaction. This key is:

1. You know the inner personality dynamics of people.
2. You have analyzed your own personality dynamics [which you probably have done by now].
3. You can read, sort and understand other people.
4. And you can communicate and cooperate in a »joining-forces«, similarity-based way with any – what so ever different – personality type.

Cooperation between different people is a guiding principle of the neuroscientist Professor Gerald Hüther. In his book »Co-creativity and Community« [1] he describes ways to act jointly and shares the following basic insights:

Our brain with all its neuronal processes serves to unfold our potentials. That sounds reassuring at first. It is, however, the entrance into the world of contradictions, challenging tensions and forks in the road. No brain works alone. It is constantly connected to other brains, which interact with each other. No living system exists on its own. It is always connected with other forms of life and can only live and develop in the midst of others. The consequence is: Nobody can develop his potential alone. Every person always needs relations and interactions with others.

Potentials are not being unfolded through competition. Competition leads to specialization and improved utilization of existing resources. Something really new cannot be created this way. Unfolding potentials is only possible through cooperation, especially with a wide range of co-creators. Hüther says it like this: »The only strategy that enables a continuous, unhindered and undisturbed development of the potentials created in a living system is the constant adjustment and readjustment of the relational patterns established within that system to changing conditions, maintaining as close and varied relationships with as many other and diverse living organisms as possible. [Page 69]«.

Thus, the success of humans lies in its collective diversity. This is constituted, among other characteristics, by the five personality types described so far. The consideration of each single trait is the *first stage of* collective diversity. At the *second* level, we find that people rarely have only one distinct trait. They always enjoy combinations. The numerous possible combinations of these five basic structures lead to a vast collective diversity. Here we find the deep cause for appropriate treatment of people and their secret of success as species.

There are two forms of appearance: external and internal. EXTERNAL - For example: A relationship person lives together with an order person. In such a scenario there are synergies and opportunities for the unfoldment of joint potentials, as well as contradictions and tensions. The relationship person wants to be close to the other person all the time. The order person would also like to be allowed to withdraw every now and then. The order person makes sure that all items are always in their place and easy to find, CDs are all in their proper sleeves. The relationship person likes it cozy. Sometimes socks and reading glasses are spread around the sofa in the living room. It may also happen that some CD cases are empty. Or that there is a wrong CD in the sleeve. This can lead to tension and conflict. We will talk about the possible synergies in a moment.

INTERNAL - There are also combinations of personality traits within individuals. For example, a relationship person could also have a strong order trait within himself. The possible synergies, but also the possible contradictions and tensions that can arise externally between different individual people, now appear internally in a single person.

Both manifestations lead to similar synergies and tensions. We first look at the internal dynamics of people with multiple personality components. People rarely have a single distinct personality trait. Most common is a combination of two. Often there is a primary and a secondary trait. The weighting of different traits defines the *third level of* diversity. Two traits can be weighted in three different ways.

Let's take order and relationship as example:

- Both traits are equally developed.
- Order is the primary trait, relationship the secondary.
- Relationship is the primary trait, order is secondary.

Each of these three combinations has slightly different perceptual and experiential outcomes. It is at this point that man begins to unfold his individuality beyond the »gestalt« structure.

The prevalence of the various possible combinations follows the relation between similarities and differences of the traits within a person. This sounds a bit complicated and needs an explanatory example. Most common is the combination of relationship and order.

Relationship and Order

At first glance, differences and opposites might be the first things that stand out. People in relationship mode tend to be emotional, warm and affectionate. Order people on the other hand, are more fact-based, objective, reserved and autonomous. These are indeed significant differences. At the same time both have something fundamentally in common, which links them together. The orientation in time.

If you would ask relationship and order people to look at their lives, they would first look into the past. Why is that? Both the development of relationships and the establishment of ordering structures takes time. Thus, in both cases, the past time has a fundamental importance which is also the foundation of self-esteem. Looking back makes this visible. Looking back creates meaning and value for the present. Both personalities have this in common. This connects them. This has a stronger effect than the differences. The experience of time acts in a figurative sense like a gravitational force. Therefore, this combination is most common in individuals. On the other hand, if you asked relationship and order people how they see their future, they would probably shrug and say: »I don't know, I'm not clairvoyant.« On the contrary, for people with this disposition the view into the future is rather nebulous and sometimes filled with uncertainties and fears. If, on the other hand, you would ask an achiever to look at his life, he will tend to look forward to the future and say: »I see many goals ahead of me, there is still a lot that I want to achieve in my life.« So he's more future-oriented. If you asked him about his past, he would probably turn around, shrug and say: »It was okay, but it's over. So what? I'm much more interested in the future.«

Beware of prejudices: For the before mentioned reason, achievement-oriented individuals may be preferred for leadership roles in organizations. This sometimes leads to the weird situation that these new managers [Achievement] stand in front of their staff [Relationship and Order] and present »good news« to them by saying: »We are now making a clear cut. Everything that was until yesterday, we forget about. From now on, we only look forward.« This is indeed good news for achiever and innovators, meaning future-oriented people. People who are relationship- or order- and thus rather past oriented people, this address is perceived as disregard, devaluation and degradation. They feel hurt in their self-esteem and react immediately with resistance. This past-motivated orientation in time is sometimes seen in a negative way, especially by achievement-oriented personalities. But it is a constitutive element of the order and relationship person and thus an important pillar of his self-esteem and dignity. Let us now take a closer look at the combination of relationship and order in a single person. How does it feel? What dynamics does this duality create inside such a person? Contradictions and tensions that would occur externally between different people occur in the same way inside individuals. The order person wants to retreat every now and then, and then his relationship part will come up and it's inner voice will say: »But it's not nice to neglect your friends now.« When this person is among friends and everyone is animatedly sharing their daily events, the order part will whisper inwardly - with all due caution and respect, of course - »What am I actually doing here? None of this really matters«. These are the famous inner voices talking to themselves. A person of this structure could be constantly torn between the two, feeling that he or she will never be able to experience and enjoy one or the other state to the fullest and thus not be able to fully develop his or her inherent potentials. But if people are aware of this inner area of conflict, they can get both parts acquainted with each other, integrate them and create synergies from these contradictions and opposites. Competence molecules with completely new properties are being created then. Order can network. Structures can bring relationships to fruition in new ways. Here is the source of abundance. This is where development and growth begin. They begin inside of each individual. This continues in interactions with others. The combination of these two personality traits is more common. In this respect, such people will more often find others who are similar to them. This provides a solid contact level where they can contribute their knowledge and experience and act together with others. They combine closeness and trust with smart and reliable thinking and acting. They are able to involve different people in their actions and thus create a larger platform for factual exchange and for positive and constructive cooperation. People with other personality preferences can be included in an emotionally appropriate and at the same time structured way.

The need for closeness and contact is rather contrasting in both personality traits. It is not so easy for pure relationship people and pure order people to come into contact with each other and to build up a relationship of trust. Combination people, on the other hand, have both parts in their personality. This polarity creates an inner tension from the need for emotional attachment of the relationship type to the autonomous factual orientation of the order type. The integration of these two opposite poles brings out the best in the other type. The order part can turn more outward and thus create an externally reflective exchange of ideas, which deepens its knowledge and experience. In this way, the order part also loses some of its introversion and social distance, becomes more visible and creative. In addition to the emotional trust base, the relationship person also gains a more structural level, which allows to take a more stable position, especially in conflicts, and not to shy away from unfavorable compromises too early. The combination of relationship and order fulfils the need for cordiality, security and fact-based and well-founded orientation, which is important for many people.

Relationship and Achievement

This combination shows greater differences between the two main preferences. While the relationship part likes to take time for personal sharing with others, the achiever and performance part quickly becomes impatient because it wants to accomplish something on the more factual level. If this inner polarity remains unconscious, the person feels inwardly torn between these two poles. But if a person consciously reflects on this, he can make both parts meet and connect and create a new inner friendship. Both traits have something in common. Deep down, they look for recognition and a secure state of belonging. At the same time, they would benefit from characteristics of the other. Due to his high tempo, impatience and sometimes tunnel-like focus, the achiever part often loses contact with others. The relationship part sometimes stops and limits itself too much to show consideration for others. When both parts combine their best qualities, this enables closeness and personal trustworthiness with clarity, process orientation and speedy action. Where pure performance orientation makes cohesion difficult, such integrated personalities can address both the emotional side of people and the need to create. This enables them to maintain and ensure the cooperation of all parties involved even under performance requirements. To the outside world, such people appear trustworthy, reliable, factually clear and focused. Warning: At the same time, people with this personality structure tend to detect and compensate for deficiencies in their environment. Here, helpfulness with a certain impatience create the drive to say: »I'd rather do it myself quickly«. In organizations this leads to compensatory behavior, so-called »monkeys on the shoulder«. The person concerned takes on tasks outside his or her agreed role and function in order to maintain the balance in the system. Wrong things are covered up by trying to better them and thus do not become visible. A real optimization of the system is prevented. Deficiency and compensatory behaviors continue. A hamster wheel is created.

Order and Achievement

In this constellation, the differences of the main preferences become real opposites. While the order part tends towards autonomy and introversion and highlights particular importance to preserving what is tried and tested, the achiever part tends to act more extroverted. He likes to be in full action with others, wants to explore new paths and simply let go of old ways. While the order part emphasizes details, the achiever focuses on fast results. He can also let things just go and let fives be straight. There are nevertheless similarities: The high level of fact and goal orientation and the somewhat reduced emotional and personal preference.

What does someone who has these two parts within him sense and experience? Someone who is not aware of this polarity might think that something is wrong with him. He oscillates between both emotionally contradictory poles and develops self-doubt. However, these doubts are unfounded. The combination is part of the plan of nature and makes evolutionary sense. The art is to create a space of possibilities from this area of tension and potential conflict. Whoever not only endures this tension, but joyfully affirms it, will experience something wonderful. He finds a solid foundation on which he can contribute his knowledge, experience and clarity and act in a goal-oriented manner towards valuable results jointly with others. He combines well-founded thinking with quick action and can maneuver safely and flexibly under changing requirements and in changing scenarios. The order part will get used to the windy airstream and the achiever part can enjoy the flow with the certainty that everything is in order and will be taken care of. The order part can dedicate its knowledge base and its good judgement to service a clear focus on objectives and the ability to act quickly. The achiever part gains more factual foundation and inner recollection. He will no longer overdose his energy and will take aim at the target flag at an appropriate speed without rushing. In this way, order and achievement mutually adjust depth of reflection and tempo and make successful action a factor supported by intelligence and focus. This compensates for the somewhat reduced emotional orientation and makes it possible to take others, for example more relationship-oriented people, along on the journey.

We had found that differences in humans stand in the way of cooperation in diversity, because people generally prefer to work with similar people. At this point it becomes apparent that it is precisely the integration of apparent opposites in a person that creates additional inner connection points and new spaces of possibility. Not only do the elements of the individual personality parts add up, but they also mutually form each other into new qualities.

This can now be transferred to the cooperation of different individuals. Different people create new qualities in the integration of their special characteristics. In cooperation, potentials become visible that go beyond the addition of existing preferences. This particular inner field of tension, initially perceived as unpleasant, becomes a real space of opportunities. This is the moment when people reach the next higher level of quality by acting together. Human characteristics are allowed to unfold without being leveled or made equal. Everyone can stay as they are. At the same time, this joint creation of new spaces of possibility also means that the individual with his or her very individual characteristics places himself or herself at the service of a superordinate whole. What is now created together belongs to all and everyone benefits equally. It is only possible with the contribution of all participants and can only be maintained as long as everyone remains involved. This creates a new field of tension. The individual takes his or her ego-focus back and becomes part of a collective mind. He becomes an individual aspect of an overall consciousness [9]. New things will emerge that individuals alone cannot create. Now potentials can unfold that were previously hidden. Suddenly, being in service is no longer experienced as a reduction of oneself, but rather as participation in something that transcends the individual experience and also enriches the individual inwardly. In this new state, growth unfolds for all who are involved in it and who are touched and moved by it. Once people have overcome this mental and emotional hurdle, cooperation becomes easy, because the more diverse everyone is, the easier it is to make connections. These are amazing revelations. Nature has earned a Nobel Prize for this.

We have now learned about the three most common personality dynamics - relationship, order and achievement - as primary preferences and in combinations of two. They can also appear in a combination of three. This is rather rare and has some surprising effects on the personality due to the higher complexity.

Relationship – Order – Achievement

The advantages are obvious: Behavioral variability, the ability to connect with different personality types and thus a wide range of positive effects in teams. We call these people »Flexible Personalities«. They think of themselves as all-rounders. They can adapt to different situations and people and can take on different perspectives. This often has a balancing effect in a team. They sometimes play the »Devil's Advocate«, i.e. they deliberately take a counter position to provoke creative contradiction. This dynamic enables variable behaviors and a high degree of positive adaptability. This is the foundation of the self-esteem of flexible personalities. At the same time, there are irritating dynamics that sometimes have negative effects. Irritations can not only occur in the person opposite, but also within the person himself.

Ambiguity

The inner radar of human beings searches for unambiguousness in the behavior of the counterpart. If the brain can quickly and reliably classify the other person, a feeling of clarity and controllability develops. The brain relaxes. But when someone meets an ambiguous personality, his radar keeps running. A feeling of blurriness and uncertainty arises. This also applies to the person himself. Many people with this personality structure report that they are unclear and confused with themselves. A self-radar is permanently running within them and it does not lock in anywhere.

Undecidedness

Making clear and unambiguous decisions is difficult for such people. The decision options are played through with all three personality parts and an inner conflict arises. The duration of the thinking process is perceived as long and contradictory due to the triple run-through. Clarity, unambiguity and decisiveness cannot be accomplished easily this way. Rather all options are kept open. In the back of the head is always this uneasiness of having to give up something else or burden relationships when a clear decision has to be made. Such people follow multiple interests simultaneously, but none to perfection. This would mean to focus on just one and let the others go. This is painful for the flex-person. Therefore, he continues his manifold path. It's like playing three musical instruments, but none perfectly. In order to play one of them in perfection, this requires to let go of the other two. For a flex-person this is almost impossible to decide.

Meet Sebastian. Suppose he has this complex personality structure and is in a dilemma. Sebastian studied business administration and currently works as confectionary chef in his parents' bakery. At the same time, he applied for a position as manager in a large frozen pizza company and was invited for an interview. Basically, he would have liked to study art history. But he did not do this in favor of his parents and their business, for reasons of reason, so to speak. For almost a year now he has a girlfriend who has opened a gallery for contemporary art and would like Sebastian to be at her side to run the gallery. If Sebastian thinks about this situation, the following inner dialogue between his parts Relationship - Order - Achievement [R-O-A] unfolds:

R: »It's really complicated.«

O: »This is what happens when you want too much at the same time.«

A: »But it's also exciting.«

R: »But how are we going to decide?«

O: »By objective criteria.«

A: »And what are they?«

O: »Well, those that in the end guarantee the income.«

R: »But all three of them do that.«

O: »But not art.«

R: »Well, sort of.«

O: »Yeah, sort of, that's what I mean. It's nothing reliable or predictable.«

A: »The gallery is cool, actually. That's what we always wanted anyways.«

R: »But the parents will be disappointed.«

A: »Well, the parents. But pastry? Is this the future?«

R: »People will always eat pastries.«

O: »This isn't just pastry. It's confectionary, gateau, cream cakes.«

A: »Okay. okay. Do confectionary and gateau have a future?«

R: »I like confectionary and cream cakes.«

A: »What about the frozen pizza job?«

O: »Frozen industrial food against confectionery? That's just ... is that a serious question?«

A: »But it is a leadership assignment in the industry. We've studied that. This has real perspectives for the future.«

R: »But the parents?«

O: »What now? We need to make a decision.«

R-O-A: »Oh, man, this is so complicated.«

Should Sebastian's girlfriend ask him how far he has come with his thoughts, he will probably say something like: »I would love to run the gallery with you, but it is all so difficult. The parents, the bakery shop, it's not so easy to decide.« An untrained observer would now think that Sebastian is weak in decision making, doesn't know what he wants, is immature, a mummy's boy. None of this would do him justice. He is quite a mature personality. He has only three strongly developed personality traits that have not yet learned to cooperate with each other. If he would structure his inner dialogue a bit more cleverly, this could lead to a completely different result ...

O: »What now? We need to make a decision.«
R: »I can't decide.«
A: »We have to. I'm for the gallery.«
O: »And why? What are your criteria?«

At this point the same inner dialogue as above takes place. But Sebastian now asks questions that create kind of an inner team building process.

Sebastian: »What is important to you?«

A: »Interesting tasks are important to me, where you immediately can see the success, as directly and quickly as possible.«
O: »I think the same way. The tasks, however, should be purposeful and require our most valuable skills.«

R: »I don't want anyone to be disappointed and that everyone can align and agree.«

Sebastian: »What strengths do you see in each other?«

R: »O — you're a smart guy. Thinking in structured ways and you are reliable. A, you are quick to the point, focused and it is fun to work with you.«

A: »Thank you, very nice. You – R – are just the friendliest of us. You keep everything together and you're always very patient. This I'm definitely not good at. But that's what you're here for. O – sometimes you're annoying with your accuracy, but in the end it makes sense. You always bring good arguments and you often have a plan.«

O: »I am precise and you – A – are fast. I find this to be an intelligent combination. R, you can do something I find difficult. You're better at dealing with people emotionally than I am.«

Sebastian: »What is your common goal?«

O: »I want Sebastian to be safe, to get a job where he can use his good talents and can continuously improve.«

A: »I want Sebastian to be able to develop and not stand still.«

R: »I want him to feel well and stay connected to the people he cares about.«

Sebastian: »What is your COMMON goal?«

O: »A job for Sebastian that matches his skills and offers opportunities for development.«

A: »Okay, agreed.«

R: »Yes, okay, but his parents and his girlfriend have to agree to it too.«

Sebastian: »But you agree with the goal, right?«

R: »Yes.«

Sebastian: »And what are the relevant criteria for your decision?«

O: »Challenging work content, good income, security and prospects for the future.«

A: »Yes. And fun.«

R: »And time for family and friends.«

Sebastian: »What is your decision now? Your JOINT decision?«

O: »Pastry shop does not meet the criteria. I don't see any prospects or opportunities for development. Neither does the gallery. It's certainly fun, but in the long run Sebastian can't bring in his nutrition competences. And they are highly valuable.«

A: »True, pastry shop is nice, but a dead end. Gallery's cool. But in the long run, Sebastian's competences will dwindle there.«

R: »All of this sounds right. But that means: pizza factory. And this will upset everyone, parents and girlfriend.«

O: »But he will have regular work hours and time enough for all of them. Without being entangled in family work situations.«

A: »Right. Working with family is always risky.«

R: »Oh dear. I am afraid you are right.«

A: »I suggest Sebastian conducts the interview, collects impressions and then we decide together.«

R: »Good idea.«

O: »Agreed. But he should ask smart questions so we can get as much information as possible.«

In what condition is Sebastian afterwards? He has faced his own inner reality. He had never done that before. He probably unconsciously avoided this inner clarification because he wanted to avoid the emotional dilemma of having to choose between his parents and his girlfriend. It could even be that he neglected his own interests and desires, just to avoid conflict. But now he made that clarifying step forward. In doing so, he has interrupted a pattern of thinking that has lasted for a long time. This will most likely trigger the following emotional state:

- Surprise
- Brief feeling of liberation
- Confusion
- Uncertainty
- Bad conscience

He'll wonder: »Am I really allowed to do that?« At this point, the decision about one's own career and life path no longer becomes a question of criteria, competencies and one's own intentions and wishes, but a question of permission. This sounds strange, but it is a common phenomenon when ties to family members play a special emotional role. Now, when he looks at his inner parts, they'll very likely say:

O: »Yes. You may. The criteria are clear.«
A: »Sure. Besides, there's nothing decided yet. But if the pizza factory is cool, then you go for it.«
R: »Yes [Sigh] ... we just have to find a way, to explain it to everybody.«

Permission, like any adult, Sebastian can only give himself. But even if he finally succeeds, he will feel the loss of the other options, the loss of the non-chosen. That hurts. Like choosing one out of three beloved musical instruments and letting go of the others. This renunciation is in internal contradiction to one's own need for diversity and is perceived as painful loss. It would be careless to accuse such a person of weak decision making. It is rather an inner conflict, which has its causes in the natural structure of this special personality. How can you help such a person?

There are two possible ways: Self-reflection and Ikebana. The first thing that helps is to make him aware of his special personality structure. Often the person himself does not know what's going on inside of him. If you make these dynamics transparent to him, new options for self-reflection arise. This alone already changes the inner search for solutions and opens new paths. One of these new ways is that the three different personality parts meet each other inwardly as if they were colleagues in a team. Every team building begins with getting to know each other. What is important to individual colleagues? What are their thoughts and fears? What do they need to be able to work together successfully? It is not a question of reducing or equalizing individual traits. Each trait is fully welcome. The goal is to create a joint space of interaction and to link all resources with each other. The focus is always on cooperation and the unfoldment of the inherent potentials. This combination of three makes amazing things possible. Those who have such resources can set clear goals, find structured ways to act and involve others in a friendly manner - clarity, order and heart.

A manager of an electricity company was promoted to the position of managing director. He had doubts as to whether he was even suited for this. In his perception he lacked the territorial part. He assumed that he would need this trait in order to be able to act successfully as managing director. In fact, he was a flexible personality with strong traits of relationship, order and achievement. What now? After he realized this, he sorted his actions for the first half year in the new role according to these three personality traits. He nicely got acquainted to all important employees and colleagues and step by step developed a good, stable rapport. Mutual trust developed within a short time. At the same time, he restructured the company in agreement with the employees and colleagues involved and launched a number of cleverly selected optimization projects. Then, with a stronger activation of his achievement trait, he began to follow these projects through. The target flags fluttered on the horizon for all to see. After only about 8 months he had gained recognition as managing director and before anyone noticed, the company was on a new course. Unspectacular, not particularly sexy, but with great effectiveness. Clear, structured and with connecting cordiality.

This was the first path to help a flex person: self-reflection. The second way is a bigger challenge. Book an Ikebana course. This is the Japanese art of flower arranging. The available elements are reduced to the essential. Nature is brought into the habitat of humans. At the same time, the cosmic order in which man and nature meet is depicted. The Ikebana arrangement becomes the carrier of the power that fills space and time. This can only be achieved by selecting only the most suitable leaves, branches and flowers and leaving everything else away. The power of that which one renounces flows into that which is chosen.

An Ikebana teacher celebrated his birthday and a guest brought a professional florist's bouquet of flowers. He took it, threw it on the kitchen table, cut it apart, chose two flowers and three branches and threw the rest away. The guest was shocked. The host put together the selected flowers and branches to form a flower arrangement and showed it to the guest with the words: »Which is more powerful? The bouquet or the Ikebana arrangement?«

Now the guest began to understand.

To Follow the Pull of Opportunities and Needs

When choosing a career, flexible personalities face the problem that they like a lot of things and cannot make up their mind. If they now meet a benevolent mentor who sees the potential of this person and makes a suggestion, the flexible personality type will happily agree. This often results in a career and life path that follows the pull of good opportunities rather than one's own heartbeat. With some luck, this works well, but sometimes it doesn't. Often such people realize in their midlife that they always have followed external references and actually do not know what they want for themselves. This could lead into a dead end.

Because it didn't have a capable goalkeeper, a good youth soccer team played a bad season. One of the quite successful forwards, a flexible personality, saw this, felt the vacuum and the need to fill this position well. Nobody wanted to become a goalkeeper. The vacuum persisted and created a pull. Finally, our flexible forward instinctively followed this strange pull and became a goalkeeper. This way careers suddenly take completely different directions. Of course, goalkeepers can also become successful and happy sportsmen. This one, however, did not. The decisive thing is to feel your own heartbeat and to really follow it.

If you want to help such a person, ask him: »What is it, that YOU want?«

Ambiguity and indecision often lead to self-doubt. These behavioral dynamics are not symptoms. They are completely normal, just not so easy to perceive and understand. For those who recognize this, the combination of these three personality parts is a powerful resource.

Now let's have a look at rather rare combinations.

Relationship and Innovation

People like this combine the very personal aspects of closeness and trust with a strong motivation to cross boundaries in thinking and to enter completely new terrains. On one hand, they look for harmonious coexistence and participate in community activities in a helpful and supportive manner. On the other hand, they want to give free rein to their creativity. In this way they enrich people around them and inspire them to develop their own ideas; now and then also to take courageous steps on the path of their own development. Others, especially those with a preference for order and achievement, may find such personalities rather emotional, unstable and less goal-oriented. The tension between these two personality traits ranges from the need of emotional connection to future and change-oriented freedom and renewal. The differences between these two personality traits are most evident in their time orientation.

Developing and maintaining emotionally reliable relationships takes time. For this reason, the relationship-oriented person tends to look to the past, to what he or she has experienced with others and what has led to connectedness. This has a fundamental and stabilizing significance. Accordingly, the relational component approaches change with caution and reservation. Instead, the innovation part looks ahead into the future. The past no longer interests him. His interest lies in the creative and visionary new. Changes are part of his positive attitude towards life. This can lead to inner conflicts. He may slow down his creative journeys to serve harmonious and undisturbed relationships with others, or shy away from radical ideas, although he would be able to think them further and give them form and materialization.

The conscious integration of these two parts of the personality is therefore of great importance for inner balance and development. The integration of the two opposite poles brings out the best in the other part.

The relationship part can combine his empathy and emotional abilities with a view into the future. In this way he takes away the fear of change and uncertainty for himself and others. The innovation part gains more reference to the outside world and thus more foundation in reality. This promotes the power of implementation without restricting diversity and uniqueness. Relationship and innovation form the basis for gentle growth and change processes embedded in trust. Successful expression of these dynamics leads to stability and sustainability in combination with adequate flexibility and adaptability.

An inward focus on the aspect of individuality connects both personality components. They are less interested in generally valid processes and procedures, hierarchies and forms of organizations or purely factual goals, but more in spontaneous experience. The consequence could be that they lose themselves in circles of like-minded people or in their creative world of ideas and thus fail to materialize them.

If you would like to help such a person to develop his or her potential, ask them: »What is your genuine purpose? What are your best ideas? What do you really want to share with others?« This question does not lead to inappropriate selfishness, but to a focus on one's own wishes and abilities, which can subsequently be shared with others at any time in the sense of successful cooperation.

Achievement and Innovation

This combination enables a clear focus on goals and results, as well as on new ideas and innovations. To the outside world, such people appear to be motivated by results, assertive, energetic and at the same time full of ideas and creativity. As they tend to abandon old things without hesitation, long-standing and proven processes, useful procedures and relationship structures could be lost in the course of this creative dynamic. To others they sometimes seem rather stubborn and frivolous. Their strength, on the other hand, is their ability to combine transformation and renewal with a sense of practical goals and benefits and to implement them energetically. If this type makes sure that others actually understand him – which is not always the case due to the abundance of ideas and the quickly evolving impatience if people are to slow to understand – the others can more easily go along and participate. If this process succeeds, these personalities become unusual and inspiring leaders and guiding figures. One more time, if you happen to be such a personality: you will experience two things. First you have more valuable and striking ideas than others. Second you are faster than others. The effect: after a while you feel surrounded by unsmart, uninspiring and slow thinking people. You will then become impatient and lose interest. If you happen to be their manager, you will lose them sooner or later, which in the end makes you less impactful.

Order and Innovation

This combination is rather rare. These traits are on opposite sides of the polarity scale. Differences are predominant. People with these preferences have both structured and systematic thinking, as well as the inner urge to cross mental boundaries and enter completely new ideation terrains. On one hand, they collect and preserve knowledge and thus represent the more conservative values of stability and orientation.

On the other hand, they are able to let go of the old, recognize the new and immediately incorporate it into their thought structure. They enable innovations to reach not only a small circle of early adopters, but also access larger user groups. New things do not lead to insecurity for this group of people, but to a broadening of their view of the world. At the same time their search for renewal is not destructive or chaotic, but always embedded in a logical system of order. This uniqueness and versatility often appear to be ambiguous and thus unclear to others, having difficulties to sort and understand people like this.

The tension between these two parts ranges from the more historical and conservation-oriented knowledge and experience dynamics of the order type to the future and change-oriented freedom and renewal dynamics of the innovation type. The integration of these two opposite poles allows the best to shine in the other. The order part can contribute its knowledge base and judging competence to create improvement and renewal in a structured way. The innovation part gains more relevance to reality and implementation power without having to limit its diversity and uniqueness. Order and innovation make successful action in this context a factor that is supported by structure and vision and extends the scope of thinking. Common to both personality traits is a certain mental and emotional autonomy. It is reflected in the innovation part in the desire for freedom. Such structured people have a strongly developed ability to perceive and judge for themselves, which makes them independent of others. Others may therefore lose interest. At the same time, knowledge-based creativity is always enriched and inspired by the exchange with others. In this sense, joining forces means encouraging such people to consciously turn more outwards and to establish an intelligent exchange of thoughts with others. In this way, they sharpen their innovative power and ensure reality and feasibility of their plans and activities. If they manage this well, they can become a guiding and inspirational figure for others. By establishing good contact with such personalities, you will be rewarded with reliability and many stimulating new ideas.

Relationship and Territory

This combination is also rare, as these traits are on very extreme opposite sides of the polarity scale. People with these dynamics possess both dominance and assertiveness, as well as compassion and the desire for closeness, belonging and friendliness. Setting boundaries and being connected, dominance and compassion are combined here to an unusual mixture. In contact with others, this is both powerful and convincing, protective and reliable. In the presence of such people, most others, i.e. people of order and relationship, feel safe and comfortable. This is one of the secrets of charisma. The impact of such a charismatic emanation could also be felt by yourself. Assuming you choose someone with this interesting personality, you easily would succumb to this magical and mysterious feeling of protected well-being, and the other person could then imperceptibly take the lead over your living together. This would lead to a reversal of roles that is no longer visible in that cloud of emotions. So, stay alert. Here is a parallel to Harold from the first chapter. Again, if this person happens to be a sales professional, watch out for your money.

Territory and Order

Interactions with this type of personality are not always easy. Assertiveness and structured thinking are combined here. The territory is orderly structured. The order is enforced against intruders. These two traits are fond of each other. They like to team up. We often find this personality structure in caretakers, groundskeepers, lawyers, chairmen of unions, head doctors and politicians.

In a positive sense, factually correct action is possible with a strong straightforwardness and stability. If the backs of both medals of these personality parts are joined together, it becomes strenuous for all involved. Territorial people tend to think others are too weak. Order-oriented people think everyone else is too stupid. Consequently, all of these - the »weaker« and »stupider« - meet a rather strong wall, which they first have to overcome to be able to position themselves. This strong wall is created by the inner radar, which sets a very tight similarity filter. Probably only a few will pass this radar successfully. People of this kind will usually have a very select circle of friends and acquaintances.

If you choose to live with such a personality, you too must pass this radar. You have to show that you are stable and can maintain structures in every situation in life. Then the person will feel comfortable with you. But he'll probably test it over and over again. Therefore, pay particular attention to such unavoidable tests.

Territory and Achievement

Here we have a quite similar situation. These two parts like each other right away. When the shining sides of these two parts combine, a strong dynamic goal orientation with a breathtaking airstream and unstoppable assertiveness is created. As long as others are allowed to ride on this race car, everything is fine in terms of cooperation. However, if the somewhat shadier sides of these two parts merge unrestrainedly, passengers are quickly shaken off or just run away to protect themselves. For the overall idea of »cooperation« this means that connecting of competences and thus development of potentials is decreasing. Keep this in mind. Then you can take precautions and this will not happen to you so quickly.

Territory and Innovation

In this combination slumbers the next big idea, in which the whole world should participate. They put all their eggs in one basket. »Big« and »new« are the motivating keywords for these personalities. Never a dull moment with such a person. Let them surprise you. However, keep your sense of reality awake, remain stable and connected.

You have now gained a better impression of the variety of combinations of these five personality traits. When their positive aspects are brought together, opportunities for cooperation and development unfold. However, these forces can also flow into demarcation and self-interest. People are almost always at these junctions and have to make decisions. These decision-making necessities are the driving force behind the inner developmental dynamics of human beings.

At first glance, five personalities seem to be simple to understand and relatively easy to recognize. At the same time, an infinite number of individual micro-characteristics are concealed behind it. No two people are alike. This abundance creates spaces for development of breathtaking dimensions. A glance at the many possible combinations gives us an idea of these dimensions.

Let us therefore take a look at some rather rare combinations of three.

Achievement – Relationship – Territory

Let's get back to Harold, whom we have already met at the beginning. He is constantly on the move, knows his way around and is always willing to lend a hand. He works as employee, colleague and informal boss, all in one. Runs a small catering service with his wife on the side and is loved and hated at the same time. You were asked if you would want to stay around a Harold? With your current knowledge, what do you think about such a prospect? Let's take a closer look at Harold. He's what we call a »jack-of-all-trades«. In him three different energy sources of achievement, relationship and territory are at work. They overlap each other effervescently, constantly connecting in a variety of ways and constantly releasing new forces. These people experience themselves as all-rounders who can do a lot, but do not want to commit themselves to a single field of activity. They are suitable for many different tasks. They are active and cannot sit still. They always have to do something, are helpful, do tasks for others quickly and gladly, and can also assert themselves if necessary. Some of them are constantly chewing on toothpicks or such. If a person like Harold would fill a leadership position, he will be perceived and experienced by people around him as energetic and totally action-oriented. A personality who does not want to dominate others or is territorially motivated, but always acts in a humane and helpful manner. These dynamics allow for variable behaviors and a large radius of action. The focus can sometimes be blurred by the overload. Other parties involved may lose the feeling of being involved on an equal footing. This behavior often leads to a lack of clarity. As a result, others cannot accurately classify such a person. They do not get a good grip on him and may experience him as unpredictable. However, since clarity is an important confidence-building element for many people, there is a risk of remaining skeptical about people like Harold. This skepticism also affects the quality of his relationships. The impression could arise that Harold's interest in relationships is only superficial. This assessment would not do justice to Harold. He himself would probably not feel valued enough, even though he is doing so much for others. He would be confused, disappointed and would not understand this.

Would you put Harold on your short-list of possible friends? In any case, you'd always have action in the house. You would deal with him in a potential-unfolding way if you use him for multi-faceted tasks, allow him many contacts and also allow him sufficient periods of reflection and rest. You may also have to expressly prescribe these rest periods for him, because he cannot sit still on his own. Helpful is, with a certain amount of perseverance, to set guidelines, within which you can guide him inconspicuously, and if necessary, more clearly. After a while everybody will have great joy with each other. The dialogue, which started on page 13 could then be conducted in this way:

You:	»Harold, we need to talk.«
Harold:	[Startled] »Yes, what?«
You:	»I think we have to sort out our living together in some way.«
Harold:	»What do you mean? Did I do something wrong?«
You:	»No, of course not.«
Harold:	»Well then, that's fine. By the way, I have a great idea for next weekend. You always wanted to go with Giselle and Toby up to the peak of the Little Cow Horn in the Black Mountains with this new cable car. I already got you tickets and I made reservations for a table in the restaurant for you.«
You:	»Harold, wait a minute.«
Harold:	[Surprised and confused]
You:	»You're helpful, full of great ideas and you're fast.«
Harold:	»Right. I hope so.«
You:	»Yes. And I think that's great. This is a very great enrichment for all of us.«
Harold:	»I am glad. But it sounds like there is a 'but' coming now …«
You:	»No. No ifs and buts. You are a great guy.«
Harold:	»Huh, then everything is alright, yeah?«
You:	»On one hand, yes. And that's a big yes. And there's another side of the coin.«

Harold:	[Surprised] »What?«
You:	»It's not easy to find the right words. It may sound strange. My impression is that you are doing too much.«
Harold:	»Ahh, what too much?«
You:	»Example: the tickets for the cable car.«
Harold:	»Yes?«
You:	»Well, what do YOU think?«
Harold:	»That was meant to be nice and helpful.«
You:	»Yeah, sure, I can see that right away.«
Harold:	»Was that too much?«
You:	[Shrugs questioningly]
Harold:	»Should I have asked you before?«
You:	»We're getting closer.«
Harold:	»You think I'm too perky?«
You:	»No. I think it's good that you're so ... ... briskly ... wait, we sort this out. You want to be helpful, right?«
Harold:	»Yes, sure.«
You:	»Then how about first checking if there is someone who is in need of help. And then you might want to ask him if he'd like to be helped at all, right?«
Harold:	»Hm.«
You:	»You grumble. What do you mean by Hm?«
Harold:	»I like to do something, want to get things moved and have some impact.«
You:	»Now you're evading.«
Harold:	»What?«
You:	»That's not the point. That you are active and get involved in all sorts of things, is one of your strengths.«

Harold:	»You think I should do more ...? ... Well ... what actually?«
You:	»Harold, you're really are a firecracker. You don't even notice yourself what we are talking about, do you?«
Harold:	»Some people say I am too dominant. Is that what you mean?«
You:	»What do they mean, when they say that?«
Harold:	»Well, I just do things without asking.«
You:	»Right.«
Harold:	»I thought that was good. Proactive and ... you know.«
You:	»Look, I don't want to string you along. You're a great guy. And now ... take a look at me.«
Harold:	»You're a great guy too.«
You:	»Thank you. Right. Do I look needy to you?«
Harold:	»No, of course not.«
You:	»Can I decide for myself with whom I want to go where and when?«
Harold:	»Yes, sure.«
You:	»And what does that tell you?«
Harold:	»That you like to do your own thing.«
You:	»Right. Just like you, right?«
Harold:	»Actually, yes.«
You:	»This we have in common.«
Harold:	»Yeah, right on. I see that now.«
You:	»Good. Harold, my impression is that you in all your helpfulness and with this drive to get things done, you sometimes cross some borders.«
Harold:	»You mean I roll over others?«
You:	»Yeah, could be perceived like that.«

Harold:	»I've heard that before.«
You:	»And does that ring a bell?«
Harold:	»There must be some truth in it.«
You:	»So what are you going to do about it?«
Harold:	»I pay more attention to what other people really want?«
You:	»Sounds great. So, what are YOU and ME going to do?«
Harold:	»Talk first?«
You:	»Good idea. Agreed?«
Harold:	[Relieved] »Agreed. And the tickets?«
You:	»We use them, of course, and have fun. And next time we'll do it differently, okay?«
Harold:	»All right, okay.«

You did it.

Another complex personality that can quickly become a challenge for others is the following combination.

Territory – Order – Achievement

Here, the dominant parts of a janitor are mixed with razor-sharp perception, crystal-clear goal orientation and persistent assertiveness. It is extremely fascinating to observe this type of personality in the free wild. His relational part is hardly visible behind this dominant triad. Only people who have passed his scan will be able to enjoy this hidden and unseen part of relationship. Then there are moments of warmth, care and above all protection. No one should even think of harassing or threatening friends and family of such a personality. Then he would experience how clarity, accuracy and territorial assertiveness can become an unimagined arsenal of weapons. The scan is only passed by people who, firstly, do not falter, secondly, have a clear sense of structure and order in detail, can behave impeccably, at the same time assert their interests and - thirdly - in the end create something valuable. Many will not pass this scan alive. For beginners in interacting with people and joining forces, dealing with this personality type is rather unsuitable. Here someone is needed who already has experience and is able to create a high degree of similarity. In the event that such a personality has reached this point in reading this book - which is rather unlikely -, we would like to conclude our observation in a positive way. Our initial thoughts were that humans are sensitive, contradictory and endowed with amazing abilities. Well, this type is insensitive, resistant and robust. But deep inside he is sensitive to those who have passed his complex and very precise scan. Then he gets soft. Then he uses his strengths, such as his detailed knowledge and impact motivation, to achieve big goals. The big goal, the Big Picture, is the form through which the contradictions of these three parts combine to form a common stream of power. Then his abilities and potentials unfold. What he should then still lack in order to manifest the great goal, he gets from others. He constructs spaces in which as many people as possible work together, in which their abilities are combined and great ideas become reality. This is indeed fascinating to observe.

Finally, a small example from private life of such a personality type. Concert night. Second row seat. Middle. First place at the center aisle. Plenty of room around him. Close to the musicians. They enter the podium and sit on their chairs with their instruments.

His scan moves back and forth meticulously. Then these comments for his companion follow.

»You see this? The violinist has unkempt hair. They're all split. Doesn't anybody see that? Doesn't the conductor pay attention?«

»They're all wearing different clothes. All black, but not tuned. Messy. Surely this does not do justice to the occasion.«

»And the shoes. Look at the shoes.«

»Who are all these different people? Look, everybody dresses differently. I don't think they'll even notice. They're probably just here for the music. Artists, actually.«

»What do musicians earn, do you know?«

»For the pianist, they don't even have a decent stool. Look. She must sit on a simple conference chair. How careless.«

»They probably save money everywhere. No money.«

»Let's see if the conductor gets everything under control.«

At the end of the concert there was a small heart moving moment.

»The music was pretty loud. The singers hardly had a chance there. But never mind. That violinist over there, the first one, he was great. That close, I could hear him clearly. He, at certain moments, played very, very fine. I don't think anyone back there in the last rows could hear that. That was very nice. Very special.«

That's how they are. Everybody's kind of lovable in their own way, actually.

This first insight into the inner life of people has created a roadmap that gives us orientation for the way ahead. However, this map is not yet complete. So far, only the basic features of the different positive forces of human beings are depicted on it, especially the personality parts in their authentic forms. We mainly have looked at people in their relaxed states, in their comfort zone.

In this state the special six abilities of humans freely unfold:

- Elasticity and resilience
- Sensitivity and empathy
- Self-reflection
- Transferability
- Anticipation
- Cooperation

When people get under stress, sensitivity turns into a kind of hyper-squeamishness and the positive dynamics start to falter. An often tunnel-like self-reference develops, empathy decreases, external perception and self-reflection are reduced. Consequently, transferability and anticipation narrow down to ego-focus and selfishness. Cooperation becomes almost impossible in this state. The development of existing potentials slows down to a standstill. This process happens very often. Successfully living together with a person is only promising if we understand their stress behavior and can deal with it properly.

Part 2
The Sensitive Inner Life of People

Humans are sensitive. They are exposed to many stressful situations in the course of their lives. It is likely that humans have developed this sensitivity due to evolutionary reasons, precisely because of the constant challenges they have to face and manage. Fine perception and empathic feeling serve to assess life situations and other people and to optimally align one's own behavior accordingly. At the same time, we observe that people leave their positive comfort zone under pressure and stress. Authentic personality parts decrease and subordinate parts are activated. While this increases the focus, it reduces the variability of action and costs additional energy. Occasionally, authentic personality traits are also exaggerated and overemphasized. Strengths then become weaknesses. Sensitivity turns into touchiness or over-sensitivity. The knack for details turns into a scalpel and a threat to others. Tempo turns into the speed of light and others can no longer follow. There is a fine line here. For example, when performance people come under pressure, they usually become faster. However, they rarely reach their targets faster. They are more likely to lose contact with others, joint thinking and acting decreases, the perception narrows, the fine adjustment of one's own behavior according to the situation is taken over by the stress driven autopilot. The stress does not decrease, but rather increases. The achiever finds himself in a dead-end road.

Order-people under pressure usually become more precise, more detailed and their already sharp perception becomes a weapon. The consequences are the same. Cooperation becomes more difficult, securing one's own position comes first and the variability of behavior decreases. Astonishingly quickly the person reaches the limit of his resilience. If he does not succeed in pausing at this limit, his positive interaction abilities will sooner or later collapse.

Let us take a closer look at behavioral changes under stress using the example of Oscar. He is a friendly person, member of various charitable associations and very sociable. At the same time, he is reliable and likes to take responsibility. Structured processes and thoughtful action are important to him. He is a person with the primary personality traits of relationship and order.

If we now look at his full profile in detail, we reach the *fourth level of* collective diversity [see above pages 76-77]. All five traits have an individual effect. A *fifth level* is created by the fact that similar characteristics can have different levels of energetic charge. We recognize in Oscar's authentic comfort zone the following distribution and charge of his personality traits.

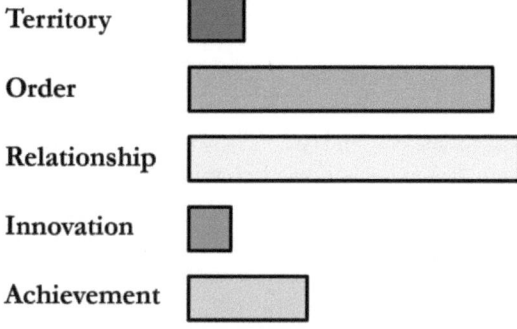

Oscar's relationship part is predominant to his order part. Both stand out clearly in comparison to all other traits. If Oscar is under stress, the emotional charge of his personality parts changes in the following way:

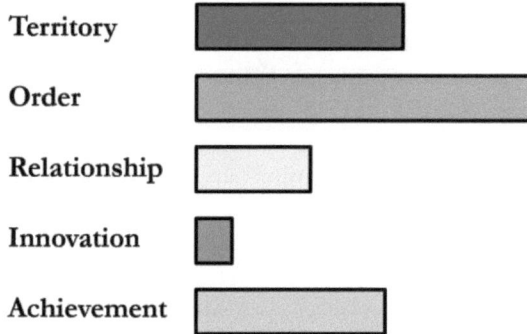

Three aspects become visible. The territorial or power trait is getting stronger. The relationship part decreases. The order trait becomes even more evident. Under these circumstances it gets sharp as a knife. Oscar becomes more critical and dominant. He puts aside his need for good relationships, puts his need for order in the foreground and bundles his forces to assert himself. This is not a consciously chosen behavior. This behavior is generated by Oscar's autopilot. Instinctive and stress-related. It serves evolutionary-based acute danger prevention. However, people also react in this way in situations that do not represent any danger at all, but »only« trigger the famous »red buttons«. This happens especially when people have become over-sensitive. They then no longer distinguish between real danger situations and everyday stress.

Imagine Oscar on a business trip. He takes the train to the airport in the morning. The train is packed with commuters. He could not find a seat. He must stand surrounded by strangers for twenty minutes. People who cough, sneeze and play music so loud despite headphones that Oscar can't avoid listening. In addition, there are those who make loud phone calls in crowded places. When Oscar arrives at the airport, he has already lost access to his authentic comfort zone. His relationship trait has retreated, his nervous radar is running at full speed and his dominance trait has taken guard duty. In this state he has to queue at the security checkpoint for ten minutes, again surrounded by people coughing and talking on the phone. A little later he sits on a middle seat in the plane – 31.1 inches seat pitch, 16.9 inches seat width. Oscar is in stress mode.

Suppose you meet Oscar after his flight in the arrival hall of the airport. You meet him for the first time and do not know the events of his last three hours. His behavior is rather demarcating and unfriendly. At this moment, it is very easy to make a wrong judgement. Based on your observations, you might assume that Oscar is a territorial personality. To connect with him you choose the strategy of similarity and address him with the words: »I see the plane was too small for you. The next person you meet is in danger.« A territorial person would grin and answer: »Right on. Good for you to recognize it. I'll make an exception for you. I keep you alive.« You would instantly connect and everything would be fine.

But Oscar is not a power person. His territorial trait is not very distinct. He is a relationship and order person. However, he is in stress mode and at this particular moment he cannot find access to his authentic personality state. He hears your words, is confused for a moment and thinks, »What is he talking about? How does he dare?« The words chosen because of the wrong judgement do not trigger a feeling of similarity, but are understood by Oscar as a reinforcement of his state of stress. Your words should signal to him, »I'm like you. We are similar.« But he understands it as: »I am just as stressed as you are and ready for quarrel«. You wanted to create similarity and rapport, you have achieved conflict and separation.

For this reason, conscious encounters with people always begin with the following inner questions and decisions:

- Is the person in his comfort zone or in stress- or conflict mode?
- If he is in his comfort zone, create similarity.
- If he is in conflict mode, immediately de-escalate.

Get him out of the stress state. It could sound like this: »I see that the journey with all these people was a strain for you«. He will probably sigh and start relaxing. If he finds his comfort zone again, intensify the similarity. »May I make a suggestion? Shall we have a cup of coffee first and put this whole thing behind us?«

The differentiated perception of the type and the distinction between comfort zone and conflict zone is important for establishing rapport, for successful cooperation and joint unfoldment of potentials. Joining forces starts here.

In the following chapter, let us take a closer look at stress and conflict behavior of the various individual personalities.

07
Ronald the Order Person

This is the story of Ronald. He is an order person. Logical thinking and criteria-based decision-making are important to him. If a proper and attentive distance to him is maintained, if his need for personal space is respected, he will feel understood and treated appropriately. Stable structures and secure mental coordinates are his basic needs to have orientation at any time. If he notices that you see and recognize these needs, he will carefully build up trust in you – with all due caution.

What does Ronald experience and how does he react when his needs are ignored and disregarded? Suppose he was often treated disrespectfully and hurtfully in his private life. Others came too close to him, harassed him, made fun of him and called him smart-ass, nerd, loner. Then they ditched him and ignored him. This led to the fact that he withdrew more and more into himself. His willingness to get involved with others decreased. He became a loner and his view of his social environment became more and more critical. This continued in his professional life. Ronald began to look for faults and failure in others; especially regarding his numerous superiors and managers over the years. His scan was particularly precise and focused on the properties »What competencies do they really have?« and »What do I benefit from them?« Anyone who has ever scanned his own superiors for these factors knows what is going on in Ronald. We all do. As a manager you have to be aware of this particular scan and better answer it in a satisfying way. Otherwise people won't follow you. Of course, he always had an eye for details and right or wrong, good or bad. However, the negative sides now came more clearly to the fore. He saw the good and positive less and less. Instead, he collected mistakes and failures of others. Like pointed arrows he put them in a quiver. He became a critical observer with an overflowing quiver of sharp weaponry.

Ronald will shoot these arrows someday. Nobody can predict, however, when this will happen. With every shortcoming or mistake he discovered in others he felt better, more correct, more superior. He began to compensate for his lack of appreciation by rising above others inwardly. Order-oriented people react in this way to violations of their self-esteem, their dignity. Their highest values are knowledge, experience, autonomy and respect. This is the basis of their self-worth and this is where they are particularly vulnerable.

It is precisely here that Ronald's sensibility has turned into over-sensitivity. This is his weak point, his red button. If it is pushed, a three-stage conflict process sets in. First, he repeats his point of view. If he is not heard, the second stage sets in. He repeats his point, but this time in other words, louder, more directly and perhaps with first signs of anger. This refers to his perceived impertinence that others do not listen to his knowledge and experience, to the imposition that the stupid rule the world. If he is still not heard, the dangerous third stage begins. He loses respect for the others and retreats. He looks for mistakes, collects arrows, sharpens them purposely, puts them into the quiver and waits for the right moment to shoot them.

Due to his negative experiences Ronald developed a fatal inner phrase: »I will prove you wrong«. If you recognize these signals in Ronald, appreciate him as a person, let him become part of your community in his own pace, without any pressure. Involve him in interesting tasks and enable him to make a meaningful contribution. This may take some time, because Ronald will watch you suspiciously at first. If you do not let yourself be diverted from your path, he will continue to look at you in disbelief for a while. But then he will understand that you are serious and you will gain a friend who may not always be easy, but who is definitely very loyal.

Self-esteem and Respect

People are very sensitive to disrespect and disregard for their self-esteem. This is a very sensitive point and one of the main causes of conflict and resistance to cooperate. But what exactly do these terms mean? What kind of experiential reality is hidden behind these linguistic codes? People experience themselves in three dimensions:

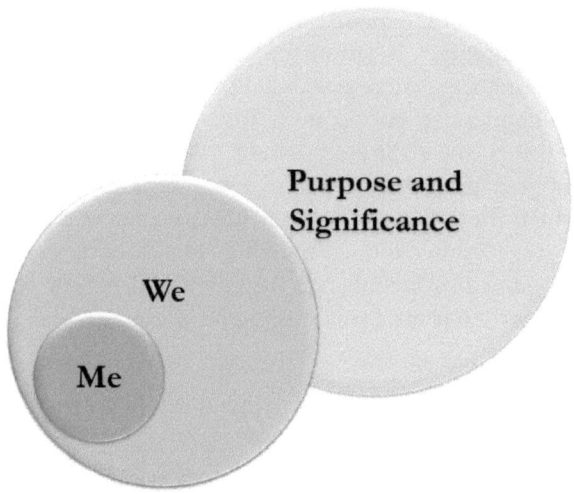

On one hand, they perceive themselves as autonomous individuals. On the other hand, they experience themselves as part of a greater overall consciousness. The brain is able to activate two different areas that represent these very opposite states. It is in this field of tension that human identity unfolds. As an individual personality he makes a contribution in cooperation with others. Potentials unfold in the we-space. A strong Me in a strong We. Buddhists say, »The purpose of life is to discover yourself and to serve others with what you found.« If one's potentials become visible and manifest, the own contribution gains significance. If these three dimensions can be successfully combined, a person's self-esteem is fulfilled and their comfort zone becomes a space of strength. A power-chamber. The dignity is then indeed untouchable. If the person is denied this, the comfort zone contracts and the conflict mode expands. He is fighting for self-worth and dignity. Relationship orientation decreases. Dominance increases. Selfishness takes over. Willingness to cooperate is lost. Potentials can only develop to a limited extent. Whoever wants to support people in a positive way creates spaces in which they can meet as individuals, connect and join forces to think and act together. This sounds good at first, but it is a challenge for every philanthropist, as we can see from Tanja's example.

08
Tanya – Relationship

Good and harmonious relationships are important for Tanya, she wants to feel emotionally embedded, to share and communicate with people around. She wants to discover and feel life together with others. She is concerned about justice and she associates it with the idea that everyone should be treated equally. She does not like making distinctions between people, for example according to criteria such as knowledge, skills and performance. She would then have the feeling of not doing justice to the people as human beings and seeing them only as useful service providers. She is helpful, takes her time and is friendly towards others. When Tanya senses that you see and appreciate these qualities, she will quickly feel at home with you, give you trust in advance immediately and look for ways to help you.

At this point, however, there is a risk of more of the same. People who are willing to help often do not recognize the appropriate limits. Let us assume that Tanya's friend Simone has a dog and asks Tanya to look after it. For a weekend. From Friday to Monday morning. On Monday Simone calls and asks for another day because something has come up. Tanya gladly takes the dog for another day. A week later Tanya still has the dog. Is that still okay within the frame of friendship and helpfulness? Tanya has a hard time deciding this. It lacks clear decision-making criteria. On one hand, it is indeed not easy to draw a clear line for the appropriate time frame. On the other hand, Tanya finds it difficult to set a boundary because of her relationship-oriented personality. Tanya feels an inner dilemma. Since connection is more important to Tanya than drawing red lines - not to mention the warm feel that Tanya has developed for the dog in the meantime - she finds good reasons for herself and Simone why she should continue to keep the dog in care. By doing this, she self-justifies and excuses her own indecision. Three weeks later Tanya still has the dog. Now at least it becomes clearly visible, that helpfulness turned into a so called »monkey on her shoulder«. Monkeys are tasks that you take on out of helpfulness and then never get rid of, while another one happily enjoys his free time or unobtrusively escapes from an unpleasant responsibility. If you want to do something good for Tanya, involve her in meaningful tasks, pay attention to clearly defined areas of responsibility and protect her from the temptation to adopt new monkeys. It won't be easy for her, but she'll thank you for it.

But what happens when Tanya feels overburdened and her self-esteem has been hurt? Let us assume that she works in a position where she is responsible for the punctual delivery to customers. She is not solely responsible for this, shares the responsibility with colleagues from other departments and these colleagues do not fulfill their tasks in a timely and reliable manner. Tanya, driven by her relationship-based helpfulness has been making up for these shortcomings for six months now. She took the monkey. She is overloaded and starts making mistakes herself. Deliveries to customers were delayed. Some customers are already complaining. The sales department criticizes ... Tanya. Her boss does not stand behind her, but instead urges her to work more effectively. She tried to explain the situation to him. He just told her not to complain about her colleagues. Tanya carries monkeys and is criticized for it. She is desperate and outraged. She has discussed this with her husband. He wasn't much help either, he just said, »Don't put up with everything. Defend yourself.«

This situation is torture for a relationship-oriented person. Getting rid of monkeys means returning them to where they belong. The colleagues will not be enthusiastic about this, either dodging embarrassingly or even openly rejecting it. Tanya would have to take a strong stand and be assertive. She would have to even accept a conflict. However, her need for connectedness and belonging is instinctively the total opposite. One may think she could simply release the monkey. This would mean not to continue doing the good-natured but involuntary work anymore. But: Delays in deliveries to customers and corresponding complaints would be the foreseeable consequence. Tanya is afraid that she will have to take the blame for that. At the same time, she feels that her boss is treating her unworthily and abandoning her. She does not know how to defend herself against it and how to find her way out of this complicated situation without suffering any damage. She is not seen and appreciated as a person by her boss. There is no longer any room for joint action. Her willingness to perform can no longer be realized to the degree of quality she is committed to. Her sense of significance decreases. Her self-esteem is damaged. Tanya feels lost in such a situation, withdraws, waits. She hopes for unexpected solutions and may even develop self-doubt. Based on such experiences a defiant inner phrase evolves: »I don't want to have anything to do with you anymore, don't even try, just leave me alone.«

However, the downward overload spiral continues. The longer this lasts, the less Tanya dares to stop the negative dynamic. If you recognize such signals in Tanya, help her to get out of this state again. Clarify the responsibilities. Address uncomfortable truths. Protect Tanya from unavoidable conflicts. Back her up whenever necessary. Relieve her of self-doubt and monkeys and help her to reconnect with colleagues and customers in a clear way. Tanya will gratefully accept your help after a short moment of checking your truthfulness.

People need joint action in order to develop. They need a safe and secure we-room. Someone who can look back on an unusual life path, who was successful as Mister Universe, as an actor and finally as a politician, in other words a real self-made man, puts it like this: »I am not a self-made man. If I were to accept this role, I would simply devalue everyone who has helped me along the way and every piece of advice I have received. You might as well admit it, you can't do all this alone. Well, I certainly can't. No one can.« [10]

People Want Solutions

A quick break: People have an instinct for problem solving. You are surely familiar with the following situation. Two people talking. Georg tells Lisa about a problem that is bothering him. He wishes that someone would finally listen to him in peace. While he is still describing his problem, Lisa has already found a solution. She interrupts him and says: »Look, it's really simple. Here's what you need to do...«. People find it difficult to listen without immediately developing ideas for solutions. Perhaps your problem-solving instinct has already been activated in the cases of Ronald and Tanya and now asks: »How exactly does this work? How should I act? Which words should I choose? What happens if ...?« You may also be thinking about your own situations and looking for solutions. You're wondering: »Is there anything more concrete coming in this book?«

The answer is: »Yes, in Part 3. Be patient.«

Patience, however, is a red-button-word for the next type of personality. Before we come to the topics of behavior, language and how to act specifically, let us therefore look at the other personalities in their conflict zones.

09
Janina – Achievement

The higher the self-esteem, the more stable the personality. The lower the self-esteem, the more sensitive the person. Even the smallest disturbances then cause the most drastic reactions. You have certainly experienced the following situation. Service hotline with a mobile phone provider. Assume a performance-oriented customer who expects quick solutions and has a tendency to be impatient. He has worked himself through the call robot and finally receives an audio signal. He's already annoyed. It takes too long for him. Being pre-sorted by a telephone bot does not correspond to his perception of service quality and customer orientation. The sound signal briefly provides a moment of relief. A voice from the tape sounds with the words: »Your call is important to us. Please stay on line.« An achiever personality loses his patience at this moment. He feels degraded to an object of an obscure business machine and will angrily break off the phone call. He is more likely to change providers than to call this hotline again.

Performance people often have a very sensitive self-esteem. Janina is a good example. She speaks fast, moves fast, doesn't beat around the bush too long and likes to get straight to the point. She wants to accomplish something and, if obstacles are in her way, she quickly becomes impatient. For quiet types Janina is not so suitable. She needs action. However, she is not self-centered and also enjoys doing things together with others. She likes to give, to participate, to change something positive with her contributions and to enjoy it. She needs less emotional appreciation than Tanja. But she also needs recognition now and then, otherwise she has the feeling of doing something wrong. Almost nothing is more frustrating for an achievement-oriented personality than to find that they have made mistakes, got caught in a dead end and have to turn around and start all over again.

Let us assume that Janina was always pushed to better performance. She has been persuaded that only the best results count and she had developed the conviction that otherwise she as a person would be of little worth. She played table tennis at a club. In a tournament she reached the final and became second. She came home and her parents' reaction was, »Why didn't you win?« When she came home from school with a grade »B«, she was asked why she did not get an »A«. Nothing was enough to gain the recognition of the people around her. She was devalued as an individual, her belonging to a safe peer group was constantly questioned, she could not develop her potential without fear. Her need to do something worth and being recognized had not been fulfilled. Instead of building a strong sense of significance and developing a stable self-esteem, she started doubting herself. She began to think: »If I am not good enough, I am not worth anything.« Performance-oriented achiever then tend to resign. However, they do not react with passivity, but with greater efforts. However, if they do not receive recognition from those close to them, a spiral of performance and frustration sets in. This dynamic will continue in working life. Something amazing and often unrecognized happens here. The need for personal recognition and affiliation is projected onto the work environment. Professional role and personal needs are mixed. The inner scan of colleagues and superiors reacts with confusion and irritation. People around such a person unconsciously feel themselves responsible for the personal recognition needs of the other one. They feel obliged to something they never have committed to and therefore, they feel in a certain way abused. They feel that they have become a projection screen for another person's daily soap. From the irritation arises distance up to rejection. The efforts of the achiever turn into the opposite. The spiral of performance and frustration continues at an even increasing speed.

Janina feels the same. She always makes an effort, speaks and acts quickly, hardly takes time to listen to others in a calm manner, and in this way loses more and more contact with her colleagues. Instead of recognition and appreciation, she experiences criticism and rejection. She becomes more impatient, prefers to do tasks herself rather than involving others and inevitably makes mistakes in the end. The criticism is growing. Frustration grows also. At the same time, she too develops a fatal inner sentence: »This can't be true. I will show you«. This is where the concrete risk of burnout arises.

Seven Levels of Significance

The basis for experiencing one's own significance and strong self-esteem is to act together with others and make a valuable individual contribution. The concept of significance needs closer examination and clarification, because otherwise it remains intangible. Significance can be divided into seven levels. We can also recognize and classify Janina's condition in it. This allows a more precise self-reflection and creates options for action.

Level 1 - Giving up
The own identity is unclear. A specific purpose is missing. Relationships with other people hardly give support and are unstable. The person feels lonely and lost, suffers self-doubt, has limited strength for active action and is about to give up.

Level 2 – Giving in

Despite all the lack of meaning, everyday life is experienced as unavoidable. The person believes he cannot change anything and follows the rhythm of uniformity. Conformity creates a substitute for orientation, safety and meaning. Boundaries are becoming small habitats. He fits in with the situation.

Level 3 - Indignation

Everyday life is perceived as an imposition. However, the affected person avoids a deeper self-reflection; instead, he becomes a complainer. The imposition is externally attributed and others will be blamed. Everything outside his own small conformal habitat is critically scrutinized and evaluated. There is a strong tendency to devalue and exclude others. Righteous indignation serves the purpose of self-exaltation and compensation for one's own lack of meaning.

Level 4 - Quest

This is where thinking and self-reflection begins. This is the starting point of the transition from complaining to taking responsibility for oneself. Options to constructively create one's own life are being explored. Depending on potential and resources, different paths become visible. People recognize the choice between self-optimization and cooperation. However, self-focus is still paramount.

Level 5 – Joining Forces and Cooperating

Realizing that self-focus leads to separation and conflict, now the search for purposeful and reliable cooperation begins. Contracts are becoming a stabilizing factor in structuring life. At the same time, insecurity remains, to the point of powerlessness in the face of breach of contract and self-referential dominance. People's ambitions and moral courage reach their limits and are constantly challenged. Accepting this challenge, however, becomes a driving force to further unfoldment.

Level 6 - Serving
The experience that giving and contributing are constitutive factors of human coexistence has become firmly established. It's not only about »performance« anymore. Trust and trustworthiness become high values. Capabilities and self-confidence to maintain connections even under stress have grown. One puts oneself in a larger context. The search for meaning goes beyond the visible and material. This finds a special expression in volunteering and philanthropy.

Level 7 - Transforming
Life in the sense of a collective joint development process becomes the center of self-perception. Inner forces are perceived as a stable beacon for the path taken. Values arise from personal experience. The internal reference system serves as coordinates for connectedness and inner and outer growth. Continuously renewing oneself and acting in connection with others become regular transformational exercises. The self-centered survival mode has been overcome and is replaced by a balanced altruism.

Janina swings back and forth between level 2 – Giving in, 3 - Indignation and 4 - Quest. She has not given up, she continues to fight for recognition, to be seen and to have an adequate space for the development of her abilities. At the same time, she is caught in a so-called drama triangle. This drama triangle holds her emotionally captive. To free herself from this, she needs to pause and reflect its driving dynamics. Neither of these two – pausing and reflecting – is easy for her and above all it is painful. At this point she needs support from outside. If you want to help her, give her the impulse to reflect on herself in peace. Mirror her the dynamics of the drama triangle. Don't be too gentle with her. This could be misunderstood. She might think, »It's not so bad overall«. Janina tolerates straight talk, direct actions and you may shake her up a bit in a healthy way.

10
Henry the Territorial

Henry claims space for expansion. He wants to exert influence and is not always considerate of others. Henry triggers different reactions with his behavior. Some submit to him because they feel safe in his presence. Others feel bothered and restricted because of his rough and dominant behavior. Still others, probably most of them, are afraid of confrontations and avoid him. Consequently, for Henry people are divided into three groups: Followers, Opponents and Weaklings. He experiences himself less as part of a cooperation process than as a leader in his own cause. This makes joint action with him difficult and creates resistance.

If you would like to join forces with Henry, it is important to create a space for real togetherness. Not a room he occupies alone, but one he shares with you. This requires on your part to make this space visible again and again and to claim and fill it yourself in a way that Henry understands and respects. In this context he must learn to share space with others. The term space does not refer to an external space, but to the perceived purpose and action space you have created for yourself and Henry. Making perceived spaces visible and tangible requires presence, action, a lot of talking to each other and sometimes even negotiating. You must always maintain and demand the results of the negotiations, so that Henry is not able to evade and being hold to his commitments. This is an ongoing process. If this works out successfully, he can unfold his potential together with you and at the same time recognize that cooperation can open up even larger spaces. As promised, you will find an example of this in part 3, chapter 14, Ziggy and Henry.

If, however, he had never had such a cooperative experience, and on the contrary has experienced rejection and conflict, then Henry is constantly fighting for his self-esteem, his significance and against loss of control. He maneuvers tactically and politically, seeks allies, waits for mistakes from opponents and then fights them. The task or cause is no longer the focus of attention, but becomes a means to securing his honor and self-value. Negative dynamics start from here. The more Henry maneuvers, the more inscrutable the interactions become. The more complicated the scenarios become, the more Henry circles the wagons to prevent others from looking behind the scenes. Camouflage efforts are increasing. In the end, he does not draw significance and fulfillment from what he constructively contributes, but from the quality of his assertion strategies. But these always lead to resistance from others. This way Henry will never run out of opponents.

Whoever attacks Henrys self-worth reaps battle. His fatal inner sentence is: »I will fight you.« And he fights like a pit bull. The moment he sinks his fangs into your calf he will never let go again. In the end such a fight only has losers. Perhaps you will not succeed in freeing Henry completely from this dynamic. You can, however, ensure that he does not see you as an opponent but as a partner - and that he does not fight you. Stand in his way, hold the tension for a moment [Remember: Stepping in – Getting close – Out again] and say four magic sentences to him: »I see you're a tough guy. And I see that you can make a big contribution. This is where we are similar. The world is big enough for both of us.« Deep down inside of him, he will feel the relief, that he has found a companion in you. But he'll be reluctant to admit it openly.

11
Susan – Innovation

Susan loves freedom, uniqueness and her abundance of ideas. It's easy to make her happy. Just ask: »What's new? Got any great ideas? Have you discovered something new?« She will be happy to share all of it with you. If, however, she feels restricted or even devalued, she perceives this as threat to her freedom and even as coercion. First, as a reaction to restriction, she tries to find new ways of expressing herself, communicating, participating and contributing. If she is denied this, she begins to fight for her freedom. If this does not succeed either, the defiant sentence arises in her: »You are all too conformist for me. I'm doing my own stuff now«. Then she leaves and looks for new thinking and acting spaces and, above all, new interaction partners. Too bad and totally unnecessary. But it happens again and again because Susan belongs to a small preference group and others have difficulties to build up a sense of similarity with her and vice versa. This leads to confusion and lack of understanding, even to the degree of distance and rejection. In the end, she is mistaken for a chaotic slob. The valuable potential that lies dormant in her, is then overlooked unfortunately.

The first step

Contradictions and sensitivities of humans make joining forces a constant challenge. Potentials unfold through cooperation. They only become fully visible when different people think and act together. However, differences lead to instinctive caution. This caution often leads to dissociation, rejection and even devaluating the self-esteem of others. Under these conditions, cooperation is unlikely to achieve.

Probably many people feel the same way as the performance-oriented Janina. They oscillate between Giving in, Indignation and Quest. They do not give up, they fight for recognition, to be seen and getting an appropriate space to further develop, unfold and express their abilities. At the same time, they are in a vicious circle. Those who break this vicious circle and work their way up to the fifth level of significance are rewarded with unfolding their potentials. Here they realize that self-interest and self-optimization only leads to demarcation and conflict and they start heading to explore ways to achieve purposeful and reliable cooperation. These are ambitious endeavors, because it always means to overcome both one's own resistance and that of others. One will only achieve this if one is willing to take the first step. Over and over again. These first steps are connected with making the fatal inner sentences visible and dissolving them.

Order:	»I'll prove you wrong.«
Relation:	»I'll avoid you from now on.«
Achiever:	»I'll show you.«
Innovation:	»I'm doing my own thing now.«
Territory:	»I'll fight you.«

As a result, a mindful approach to self-esteem and dignity becomes possible – for others and also for oneself. It is best to take this first step as early as possible before damage of self-esteem escalates. Such dynamics often begin with a »more-of-the-same« behavior.

Beware: More of the same

You have seen it many times. A person hurries to an elevator. He pushes the button. There are no signals whether to elevator is coming or not. What does a person in a hurry then do? He pushes the button again, but harder. Over and over again. Does that make sense? No. Does the person know that? Yes, of course. We all know. He's doing it anyway. Empathy and self-reflection are partially blocked under the perceived time pressure. The autopilot is activated. Irrational behaviors are supposed to release the emotional blockage. It doesn't make sense, but nobody can suppress this instinctive behavior. We can see this pattern in all types of personalities.

An order person becomes even more precise, more detailed, more critical and less inclined to connect and exchange with others. His critical mind becomes a weapon – »I'll prove you wrong.«

A relationship person withdraws into his peer group, appeases, continues as before and waits. »Let's wait and see«, is a phrase often used. At the same time, he develops defiant defense. Defiance is the key signal, that a relationship-oriented person suffers from an injured self-esteem. If conflicts escalate to an extreme and his opponents would go down, he would probably look away – »I don't want anything to do with you anymore. I'll avoid you from now on«.

The achiever is becoming faster and faster, more direct and more impatient. He no longer has the time or motivation to find joint solutions and compromises. He can no longer pause. Through this pace and urge he will lose possible cooperation partners – »I'll show it to all of you.«

The territorial or power person takes over the space, gathers allies around him and increases control. He casts a shadow in which hardly anyone can grow. When stress and conflict escalate, a battle begins with no expectation for compromise – »I'll fight you«.

The innovator does several things at once. He produces new ideas and fights against constraints. In this field of tension, he begins to swing back and forth hysterically and without orientation. Until he gets enough. Then he leaves. Freedom prevails – »I'm doing my own thing now.«

For »more-of-the-same«, watch these two Scottish guys in an elevator with voice recognition on YouTube »burnistoun voice recognition elevator.« You will get a laugh attack and you will never again push any elevator buttons anymore.

There is another example from the world of business: The Mercedes-Benz S-Class W140, the

»Helmut Kohl S-Class«, from 1991 [Helmut Kohl was a big guy and German chancellor from 1982 – 1998]. Managers always start their careers as experts. They then become team leaders. Team leaders become Managers of team leaders and so on. Some make it from apprentice to chairman. Often such people have a personality structure which is rooted in Territory, Order and Achievement [see page 109]. Such a personality type was the responsible CEO for developing the W 140. He was about to retire from the company. The pension was just around the corner. A territorial, order and achiever person, with a seniority of more than 40 years facing retirement – not a good moment in life. What goes on in such a person's mind? »Great, it's over. Finally, some free time. Growing flowers in my garden«? No, I don't think so. It is more likely that discomfort and fear will spread out within him, fear of approaching meaninglessness, loss of significance. Such a person wants to have an impact beyond his time. He wants to make himself immortal. He wants to create a monument to himself. Eventually he is developing a vehicle like the W 140. Not focusing on customer's needs or the market demands, but only on himself. What did everyone else say? Nothing. They applauded. Nobody dared to stand up against his narcissistic decisions. Territory, Order, Achievement. Better not argue. Danger.

The W 140 was a giant. Big. Defiant. Swank. Over five meters long, almost 1.90 meters wide, 1.50 meters high and weighing 2 tons. The first vehicles did not fit on motorail trains because of their width. With four people on board, it reached its maximum permissible weight. Just more of the same. Even German Mercedes drivers were embarrassed by this vehicle.

Sales figures fell dramatically and did not recover as quickly even with the successor model. Today it has almost completely disappeared from the streets. BWM probably celebrated a huge party.

You got introduced now to five personality types in different combinations. You can distinguish between authentic mode and conflict mode. You can perceive and classify self-esteem violations. You know that people have a strong sense of purpose and wish to unfold their abilities and potentials in interaction with others. You want to make all of this possible for the people who are close to you. The question that is still unanswered is: How exactly does this work?

There often is a concern. What do I do when someone meets me with defense and resistance? Some would love to exchange the person. Like stuff ordered online. Just send it back. That doesn't solve the problem, it just shifts it onto someone else.

Exchange is not possible.

Part 3
How to Address People in a Joining-Forces-Appropriate Way

In interacting with people our overall goal is: Activating the six strengths, connecting and cooperating, creating a space for unfolding the potential. How does this work?

Part 1 focused on reading people and creating similarity.

Part 2 was about getting people out of stress, conflict, resistance and guiding them back to their authentic comfort zone.

Part 3 is about choosing the right words and effective behaviors. Getting real.

12
Words are Tools

To connect with our dialogue partner, we first have to pass his inner radar. We don't have much time for this. People need no more than 150 milliseconds for a first scan [2]. Let's give ourselves a little more time now, the first five minutes. During this period, you can send the following signals:

01. I am present

So put the phone down. Don't mess around. Don't keep looking at your watch. Not being anywhere else with your thoughts. No multitasking, please. Positively speaking: full attention to the person who is facing you.

02. I see you

This does not mean that you stare at your dialogue partner or scrutinize him from top to bottom. You perceive his personality, what's important for him and convey this by choosing the right words.

03. I am cooperative and willing to share with you

You show this by exchanging information with your partner without demanding anything in return. You will talk about business later, after both of you have passed each other's scans.

04. I am interested in you as a person and not only in benefits for me

Get to know each other. Be curious. There are three magic questions that are always right and open doors:

- What is on your mind? What are your thoughts and concerns?
- What is important to you? What's your purpose?
- What are the circumstances you are currently living or working in?

05. I am appreciative and respectful

You can easily avoid the following misunderstanding. Many think that appreciation means telling the other person how great you think he or she is, what a great job he or she has done, how chic his or her new tie or scarf looks. Appreciation does not primarily refer to what people are capable of, what they can achieve or what they look like. This is easy to understand when we slip into the role of Mark for a brief moment. He works in the service center of an internet dealer. His boss comes to see him from time to time and tries to give him »recognition«.

»Hey, Mark, great job«
»I must really praise you today as a model employee«
»Gee, Mark, I can always count on you«
»You always do a great job«
»Keep up the good work«

Mark, of course, was happy about it. At the beginning. After a while, his inner scan reacted, went up some degrees and became more accurate. Mark began to doubt. Does the boss see ME or does he only see HIMSELF? Is he talking to me or is he just talking to himself?

Your dialogue partner experiences real appreciation and recognition when he feels that you see him as an individual person. Everything else, such as punctuality, cleanliness and performance are secondary to the human brain. Here's what Mark would rather hear:

»Hey, Mark, I saw how you managed to get this angry customer into a real conversation. It just took you three very respectful and clear sentences. Great wording. Great effect. This was cool.«

»I can see how important the person behind the client is to you. I don't take this for granted. This creates a very nice customer experience and builds trust in our services. Thank you very much.«

06. I am transparent

I'm easy to read. I'm not hiding anything. What you see is what you get.

07. We are similar

Talk about what you see in the other person. Use matching words, similar tempo and a similar mood. Even if you are both different, show the other person that you value him as he is and that you are building bridges on which you can jointly cross towards each other. At the beginning you only meet on these bridges. Later you invite each other to your respective side and show the other person your world. New joint spaces are emerging now. Joining forces starts from here. Potentials can unfold now.

08. I got something for you

Now you can communicate what you have to offer and what the benefits are for your conversation partner.

09. You first, then Me

When two people interact, there is always this sequence. If there is a room you both want to enter and you have to pass the door, someone has to go first. This is a magic moment. The magic sequence. Always start interactions from the perspective of the other person. What is important to THEM? What is THEIR benefit? In the beginning, DON'T talk about things that interest YOU most or are important for you. Start with those that are important to THE OTHER person. First serve, then earn. This is the magic sequence in action.

10. You can count on me

Show the other person that you keep your promises. Show him you'll still be there tomorrow. Be reliable. In the end you can only make this visible by your actions, of course. You can, however, give it a boost by choosing the right words.

An example of how you can develop rapport step by step: A traveler stays in a small country inn near a large city. There he has appointments from time to time, but does not always find an affordable hotel, because trade fairs often take place and hotels then demand »trade fair prices« [hotel managers have probably never heard of the scan and how to build trust with their customers]. The country inn is managed by the owner herself. She picks up the guest from the parking lot, has registered his arrival and has met him immediately. She greets him with the following words: »I will meet you halfway and pick you up. Welcome.«

Clear words, presented accurately and politely. After some mutual greetings she continues: »I'll go ahead and you just follow me. There's the entrance, I'll check you in in a minute.« At the reception she says: »Please stand here. I'll go around the counter and then I check you in.« All very correct and proper. After the usual explanations, she adds: »You can also eat at my place. I prepare dinner myself. At 8:00 pm. It can also be 15 minutes later. I just need to know in advance. Would you like that?«

What does the guest know after these first minutes? This is a lady with a high degree of order-orientation. She is accurate, polite, responsible, loves structure and clear procedures. She also has a relationship part that cares about the guest and wants him to feel well. The guest immediately knows, here I can relax, the stay will be pleasant. He just has to behave properly.

Of course, he accepts the dinner offer. Food and service are excellent. The hotelière comes to the table and asks if everything was well. Now comes the moment to pass the scan of the lady and to connect more deeply. He finds the following words:

»I am going to turn off my cell phone.«
The lady reacts with a brief moment of surprise.

»I see you have a very special eye for details.«
The lady reacts with a relieved sigh and an inner joy for this recognition.

»The selection of ingredients, the side dishes, it all complemented perfectly and tasted wonderfully. I

get the impression you've given this a great deal of consideration.«
Joyful reaction.

»Very fine. Thank you very much.«
More joy.

Is there any way to improve on that? Yes. There always are ways to make it even more joyful.

»You know what my impression is? Not everyone can see the details you care for. I suppose most people don't have the sense for these small and subtle things.«
Deep sighing consent.

In less than five minutes a fine bridge of relationship has now been created. The lady sat down with the guest and a conversation started. A nice exchange. Each one told the other about his world. Personal, but not too personal. Still from role to role. From hotelière to guest. A perfect moment. There is a simple formula for this:

Observing + Sorting + Finding the Right Words + Addressing + Sharing = Rapport and Contact.

This applies to all areas of life. Summer. Shopping Outlet. Long queues at a snack bar and a saleswoman who is visibly exhausted, overwhelmed and on her last nerve. A customer appears to buy a bottle of mineral water.

Saleswoman: [Grumpy] »Next please.«
Customer: »I see that you've got a tough day.«
Saleswoman: [Surprise]

Customer: »It's certainly not easy for you to serve
               this crowd today. Respect.«
Saleswoman: [Sighing approval]
Customer: »A bottle of water, please.«
The saleswoman's final words: »You saved my day.«

The next person in line was served a little more friendly. Who knows what this was good for. Perhaps an escalation was avoided at the very last moment. Perhaps the saleswoman would have lost her temper with one of the next customers. This may have caused a dispute and she could have lost her job. We'll never know. This is one of the great challenges when we break negative cycles. We never know what might have been. This is called »prevention paradox«.

We must learn to act without expecting anything particular in return.

We throw a stone into the water, wait curiously for the waves and then surf them bravely.

We always have a compass: cooperation and unfoldment of our potential. Together. Joining forces. That's always right.

Another example: The manager of a »kindergarten« has a conversation with an employee who is stressed out, overwhelmed and has obviously reached the limit of her competences. This is called a serious performance review. The manager, however, moves into a different direction. Her goal: cooperation and development of existing potential.

After a few minutes of the conversation, the shortcomings are clearly on the table. Another superior would probably have issued a warning or dismissed her immediately. The following nicely chosen words set the course for cooperation:

Manager:	»We have everything openly addressed now. There are different issues clearly on the table. The question is now, how to tie this up? I would like to make a suggestion. Would this be okay?«
Employee:	[Anxious consent]
Manager:	»I have seen some good things. Three in particular. That's where I would like to connect. Are you okay with this?«
Employee:	[Relief]

The first five minutes are the space where miracles can unfold, the space where contact between people is established. These miracles begin with us. How can we judge the quality of contact? With the help of the »Contact Thermometer« we make this somewhat diffuse term more tangible.

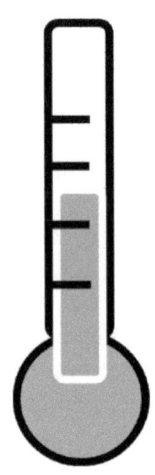

30° Friendship

27° Trust and Partnership

24° Appreciation and Respect

21° Sharing and Sympathy

18° Person and Interest

15° Function and Benefits

12° If it must be

The various degrees can be described as follows:

12° If it must be
Someone knows that he needs another person or his performance, but he finds this unpleasant. If he could, he would avoid it. But he can't. And only because of this he interacts, i.e. calling the hotline of a mobile phone provider.

15° Function and Benefits
Someone sees his counterpart in his functional role only, not as a person. He is not interested in the person. The focus is on the benefit or the necessity associated with the function, i.e. a taxi driver. The person remains interchangeable.

18° Person and Interest

Behind the functional benefit or necessity, the person becomes visible. Slight interest arises. But it is still fragile and can end any time – for example a taxi driver with whom you had a good conversation and who also drove fast and unerringly. He hands over his business card to you. Would you call him again next time? Maybe. The feeling of interchangeability decreases.

21° Sharing and Sympathy

Besides the factual level, the person becomes more important. Real interest evolves. One wants to learn more about the other person and seeks personal exchange. Sympathy arises.

24° Appreciation and Respect

Mutually deeper and more important experiences have been made. Personal benefit and gain were achieved. The other one is valued as a person and as partner in interaction. The depth of experience has created respect. The relationship started to become important.

27° Trust and Partnership

The depth of experience and commonalities have increased. Trust has developed, not only in the fulfilment of the function, but especially in the person. He is perceived as a reliable partner.

30° Friendship

The fulfilment of the function recedes into the background. The personal relationship has become more important and takes priority. A friendship has developed.

Let's take a look at the level of contact with the hotel manager, the saleswoman at the snack bar and the employee of the »kindergarten«. Try to apply the »Contact Thermometer« yourself before you continue on the next page.

Here is a possible classification:

Hotel manager: 22° - 23°
The context and the associated intensity of contact enables quick familiarization beyond the pure business transaction. Through consciously appreciative interaction on the part of the hotel guest, the degree of contact has significantly increased.

Saleswoman: 17° - 18°
Due to the short contact time and the limiting context, the degree of contact remains low. However, both personalities have become mutually visible. A short but appreciative and therefore relevant interaction became possible.

Employee: 19° - 20°
The joint work in the »kindergarten« leads to a high frequency of contact, while at the same time both conversation partners remain in their functional roles due to their hierarchical function and the critical performance issue. Nevertheless, an attempt was made to give the personal visibility more space. A start has been made. However, this new level of relationship is not yet stable. It can be lost again at any time.

To achieve a degree above 24°, positive joint experiences that have passed the trust scan are required. This takes time and relevant situations to prove its stability.

Someone might object that such sentences, as in the examples described above, would never occur to him and that he would not be that quick-witted enough. The concern is unfounded. There is a structure behind the above language examples that anyone can learn.

Observing + Sorting + Finding Words + Addressing + Observing the Reactions and Signals + Staying Tuned and Continuing Sharing.

People who know where to look at, suddenly recognize things they never saw before. It is also easy then to find the right words. You'll recognize this immediately. The catch is this: people sometimes don't dare to say these words out loud. This is an amazing phenomenon. When asked, they often give these answers.

»I don't know the other person good enough to approach him in such a direct way.«

»I don't want to offend the other person or appear rude.«

»I'm afraid this will make things worse.«

»I don't know what may happen when I address things.«

»I don't want to trigger anything that is against my intentions.«

People are afraid that if they address things clearly, they will trigger something uncontrollable. They are afraid of uncertainty and want to avoid conflicts. This is astonishing, because in the reality of these people there are usually no concrete reasons for this concern. For example, if you meet a detail-oriented person and say to him, »I see you have an eye for details«, the other person can only react in one way. He's happy.

Brains always respond to I-see-you signals with a Yes, with releasing positive hormones. Always.

Some ask at this point, »Isn't that slimy?« It is slimy when you act slimy. The other person notices this due to his fine scan and feels manipulated. Even if someone is not aware of his fine scan, his perception always works. He cannot name what irritates him, but he feels the disturbance. It's not slimy if you're authentically interested. Then the other person feels recognized. Everything depends on your inner attitude. So, you will only receive a Yes if you send a flawless »I-see-you« signal. Flawless means to be present, respectful, with the attention completely on the other person, namely on his or her identity-forming characteristics. Especially with a genuine interest in the other.

If you would say to an order person: »I see you are wearing a tie with really funny colors«, the order person's brain would be irritated for a short moment. His inner question would be, »why is he saying this?« The scan would continue running, even more agitated. This costs extra energy and feels disturbing. To address the order person in such a way would be a small inaccuracy, which almost inevitably leads to a dead end. If you would say the same sentence to an innovator, he would be happy. »Flawless« means, you want to sort the right signals to the right person before you address them. At the top of the list are the signals that have something to do with the identity of the other. These are primary signals. All other signals, such as clothing, car, leisure activities, are secondary and come later on the priority list. For an innovator, a colorful tie is an expression of his creative personality. For a person of order, on the other hand, it is rather a courageous attempt to cross borders. More appropriate phrases therefore would be these:

»I know you as a very correct person.«
»Yes, that's right.«
»And now I see that you are allowing yourself to use bright colors. Brave and chic. Respect.«
»Oh, yes, isn't it, I think so, too. Thank you very much.«

The worm must not taste good to the angler, but to the fish. And we don't use hooks, but friendly outstretched arms. This is a good keyword to dispel the myth of small talk. There is no such thing as a one-size-fits-all. So, there is not the one single small talk. Moreover, the term is not well suited to express its meaning. Small Talk is used to establish contact. It allows a space, created for a short time, in which people involved can scan and get to know each other. The better term would be »Scan Talk«. Since each personality type has a slightly different scanning strategy, there is not just one scan talk, but at least five. Suppose a person was invited to a networking event. He knows no one there. He doesn't have to, because that's why he goes there. He enters the hall and looks around. The five personality types react very differently to such a situation. You can probably already predict this. Let's single out the order person.

For the latter, a networking event is very unpleasant. He is basically somewhat reluctant to open up and communicate. He perceives small talk as a ritual without deeper meaning. What people exchange during the first ten minutes usually does not interest him. Even being subjected to such a ritual is embarrassing, intrusive and he feels immediately uncomfortable.

So, the order person has entered the hall and is looking around. There are now two possible ways in which this situation could continue.

- He approaches someone and makes contact himself.

- Someone approaches him and wants to contact him.

Let's start with the first case. Ideally, he has prepared for the event and made a small list of interesting people he could contact. The following contact process may help making it easier.

Going forth – Arriving – Going along – Taking along

In other words: approaching the person, taking a moment to really arrive and observe, creating rapport through similarity and only after you've done this, taking the lead. This is a more specific form of »pacing and leading« with the sequence: preparing – moving – pacing – pacing – leading.

In our case he recognizes one of these listed persons in another corner of the room. The other stands there alone with a half-empty glass of white wine. The first step means »Going forth«. It sounds easy, but it's not. He starts to move. Heading towards the target. As the distance decreases, his pulse rate increases. He's suddenly getting nervous. Inwardly, a fearful self-talk arises.

»What am I supposed to say when I get there?«
»What if he doesn't want to talk to me at all?«
»If he does, what shall we talk about?«
»What am I doing here anyway?«
»How have I gotten myself into this?«

Fear is increasing. Fear of rejection. Fear of unintended responses, of uncertain outcomes, of embarrassing failure. Every contact begins with »Going forth«, with approaching the person. This is probably the greatest deed a person can do, because he has to overcome many inner very personal resistances and fears. Sometimes it's as bad as bungee jumping. You let go and hope for the best.

»Arriving« means to look, see, observe, scan and sort. What type of personality is he? Is he comfortable or is he uncomfortable with the situation? What were the motives that got him to this event? What signals does he send?

»Going along« means aligning, pacing and creating similarity. I see you, and what I see I find interesting. It also means to become visible oneself, to let oneself be seen by others and to pass their scan. Small talk equals scan talk. Such a moment could take place as follows.

»Hello, may I introduce myself to you?«
»Of course, that's what we're all here for, isn't it?«
»That's right. I feel a little uneasy about this.«
»I understand that. But you did.«

»You make it easy for me.«
»Here you go.«
[…]
»By the way, why did you pick me of all people to talk to?«
»That's a good question. I had you on my list.«
»What? You have to explain this to me.«
»With pleasure. I've heard about you before and I was interested.«
[…]

Now ideally an exchange begins, a mutual »Going along«. Sharing. After a while, the last step on this contact path comes, the »Taking along«. If you go to a networking event, you have a goal, you want to achieve something with someone else. Now is the time to address it and to do this clearly.

»First of all, I would like to thank you for this friendly conversation. And at the same time, I have a request. May I be so direct?«
»Go ahead.«
»My intention is … What do you think?«

For relationship-oriented people this scene feels perhaps a little too formal. But it was meant for order people. There are five different types of small talk. And through this example we now know how to address an order person. This was, however, a positive example. But sometimes, as some may be afraid of, a conversation may not work out so well. What if the other person doesn't make it easy for you?

»Hello, may I introduce myself and talk to you for a moment?«

»I don't know yet.«
»I notice you're very careful checking who to talk to.«
»Exactly.«
»Did you make yourself a list?«
»What?«
»With the people you're interested in talking to.«
»No.«
»I have.«
»What?«
»A list.«
»So?«
»You're on it.«
»Eh?«
»I realize I'm only disturbing you. Such was not my intention. I didn't mean to be intrusive. I'm going to go back to the bar and get another glass of wine. Goodbye.«
»Hold on.«
»What?«
»I'm interested in this list of yours.«
»Should I bring a fresh glass of wine for you, too?«
[…]

People often think in such fear-driven scenarios. What should I do if something goes wrong? Let us therefore look at a situation that has actually failed.

We have stated before that you always get a Yes when you send a flawless I-see-you signal. Flawless means being present, respectful, attentive and genuinely interested in the other person. If you are not careful, you run the risk that the sensitive scan of your counterpart will immediately report the deviation as a fault.

A passenger gets into a taxi. He looks around and realizes that the taxi is very old and not very well maintained. After a few moments he thinks: »Why do I have to get into such a dirty old thing?« Discontent arises. Now it's best not to say anything. But the passenger has the impulse to address this.

Passenger: »I see your car already has a lot of miles on its meter.«

Taxi driver: »If you don't like it, you better get out again quickly.«

What went wrong here? First, the passenger had an unfavorable »mindset«. His goal was not cooperation but criticism. Actually, he wanted to get out of the car as quick as possible. His aim was not to start but to end the cooperation. The taxi driver's brain noticed this immediately. He probably knew himself that he should not carry passengers in this car any more, was already stricken in his sense of honor and hypersensitive and noticed the displeasure of the passenger immediately. His scan responded spontaneously.

Secondly, a secondary characteristic was addressed, the car, not the person. The brain responds to I-see-you signals with a Yes only if you send flawless signals and words. These refer exclusively to person and identity and have cooperation as their authentic goal. Then you are on the safe side.

13
Don't Be Afraid of Addressing

A good interaction begins with an I-see-you signal. This is always a safe starting point for a conversation. But then what happens next? Let's take another look at Janina, the performance-oriented person. She is under stress, is impatient and loses contact with her colleagues. Her boss would like to address and solve this. For this purpose, he combines the existing strategies and tools.

1. Going forth:
Making the first step

2. Arriving:
Observing – sorting – finding words

3. Going along:
Addressing – creating similarity – exploring and sharing

4. Overcoming resistance:
Addressing – creating self-reflection

5. Opening a fork in the road:
Getting a Yes for dialogue

6. Taking the lead:
Engaging in dialogue – getting a Yes for solutions.

This is the guideline for the interview with Janina. The boss starts with an I-see-you signal.

Manager:	»Hi Janina, can I get to the point right away?«
Janina:	»Of course.«
Chief:	»I can see you're pretty stressed.«
Janina:	»Well, you see a lot. It would be even better if you would do something about it.«

Not every I-see-you-see signal triggers happiness and consent. Sometimes it brings unpleasant truths to the surface and creates sudden resistance. In such cases simply use ...

The 4-Phrase-Strategy

Manager:	»Hold on. I'll start all over again. I know you as an employee, to whom it is important to come to the point, not to talk too much but getting things done quickly and to deliver results.«
Janina:	»Right.«
Manager:	»I can see that.«
Janina:	»Nice of you ... and what now?«
Manager:	»And I appreciate this very much. I find this really very cool.«
Janina:	»Huh.«
Manager:	»At the same time, I see that you're struggling and that you are wearing yourself out. And that's what I want to talk to you about today.«
Janina:	»Huh.«
Manager:	»I hear you making noises. Are you okay with this?«

The structure of this 4-Phrase-Strategy consists of the following elements:

1. I see you / I perceive you / I feel something / My impression is

Manager: » ... I know you as an employee, to whom it is important to come to the point ...«

Please pause a moment for the sentence to take effect. Wait for a reaction from the other person, before you continue.

Janina: »Right.«

2. I appreciate you / I understand you / I want to understand you / How this affects me

Janina: »Nice of you ... and what now?«
Manager: »And I appreciate this very much. I find this really very cool.«

The resistance in Janina's answer is ignored by her manager and he continues unwaveringly with the second step. Leave a pause for the sentence to take effect. Then wait again for a reaction from the other person.

Janina: »Huh.«

3. Taking the lead and moving on to the topic

Manager: »At the same time, I see that you're Struggling ...«

Another pause, wait for reaction.

Janina: »Huh.«

4. Closing question

Manager: »I hear you making noises. Are you
               okay with this?«

He mirrors her reactions and then formulates his
closing question. The idea behind this strategy is: No
leading without contact. The first two phrases serve
to create rapport. Only then you can take the lead
followed by the final closing question. But what
happens if Janina doesn't want to cooperate and her
resistance continues?

Janina: »You know yourself, we are
               understaffed, people are missing
               everywhere, customers start pushing,
               some colleagues don't even bother
               much, and, and, and, and.«

Janina avoids the subject. The solution: repeat the 4-
Phrase-Strategy. First sentence first: I-see-you.

Manager: »Janina, I notice you're avoiding the
               topic now.«
Janina: »What?«
Manager: »You're sneaking out.«
Janina: »What do you mean?«
Manager: »I am talking about you and your
               stress behavior. You distract from that
               and talk about working conditions
               and colleagues.«

An I-see-you phrase signals an extra dimension. It also sends the message: »I see everything.«

Janina:	»But it all belongs together.«
Manager:	»You say, it all belongs together. That's true, of course. At the same time – if we look close enough – these are two different topics. And these two things I would like to separate for today. Is that okay?«
Janina:	»Huh.«
Manager:	»You always make these noises. What do you mean by 'huh'?«
Janina:	»Huh, means, that I notice that you don't want to talk about the work, but about myself. But you know, I am who I am.«
Manager:	»These were two sentences. So, let's sort this out. I don't want to talk about the work today. You got this right, spot on. This tells me, that you're wide awake and clear in mind. This is how I know you. And that's great ...«
Janina:	»Here you go.«
Manager:	» ... the second sentence was 'I am who I am'.«
Janina:	»Right on.«

Now follows the second part of the 4-Phrase-Strategy: »I value you.«

Manager:	» ... I think you ARE great the way you are.«
Janina:	»Oh?«
Manager:	»Do you buy that?«

Janina:	»Actually, yes.«

Now follows the leading sentence, moving forward to the actual issue.

Manager:	»Good. That's why we don't talk about the way you ARE.«
Janina:	»Then what?«
Manager:	»Hey, you really give me a hard time today.«
Janina:	»Huh?«
Manager:	»You see me sitting here in front of you trying to have a decent conversation with you.«
Janina:	»Huh.«
Manager:	»And you string me along.«
Janina:	»Well, it's a stupid topic.«
Manager:	»And now I'm looking for the right words.«
Janina:	»Huh.«
Manager:	»Actually, you know yourself what we are talking about.«
Janina:	»Stress.«

Now comes the closing question, or rather the invitation to the conversation, to a genuine dialogue.

Manager:	»Right. Tell me more.«
Janina:	[Silent and thinking]
Manager:	[After a moment] »What's on your mind now?«
Janina:	»Okay. So ... «

As we see, it is quite appropriate to expressly address what you recognize in your conversation partner. His scan will report: I am seen. If, in addition, it is possible to find the right words to reflect the inner process of your counterpart and to signal appreciation, his scan reports: I am not only seen, but also understood and recognized as a person. Now, contact is established. In the very same way, you can address and dissolve resistance and create a genuine dialogue and sharing.

A little extra trick:

You can also accompany verbally what you are doing and what is going on inside of you. In this way you make yourself and your inner processes transparent to the other and become easier to read. The scan of the other person relaxes and contact is more likely to be established. However, addressing of the obvious is what may feel strange, although it makes it easier for the other one's brain to scan you.

Manager: »You see me sitting here in front of you and me trying to have a decent conversation with you. And now I'm looking for the right words.«

As strange as it may feel, it is a strong rhetorical maneuver that sometimes can even save us from difficult and embarrassing situations. In May 2009 there was an amazing example of this, which probably nobody noticed because millions of brains had relaxed at the same time. It is a German example. The German Federal President at that time, Horst Koehler, was about to be re-elected for his second term of office. The election had already been decided beforehand and the members of the Federal Assembly were therefore already in place together in the plenary hall of the Parliament Building, the German Bundestag, at an early stage. Only Horst

Koehler was not there yet. He was still in Bellevue Castle, his official residence opposite the Parliament, and probably thought he should wait a little longer.

At that time Ulrich Deppendorf was head of the city studio of one of Germanys major TV channels and reported live from the election. He was at his reporter's desk in the lobby of the German Bundestag. However, all possible interview partners were already in the plenary hall. No one was left to talk to on live TV. Horst Koehler did not come and the cameras of the live broadcast were pointed at Ulrich Deppendorf. That was an embarrassing moment. Now, he made the following: He accompanied verbally what he was doing and thinking. This sounds weird, but it worked miracles.

»I'm standing here in the lobby of the German parliament. As I can see, and you can see this on your screens at home now, the lobby is deserted. All members of the Federal Assembly are already gathered in the plenary hall and are waiting for the decisive moment of today. Above all, they are waiting for the appearance of Horst Koehler. I now leave my desk and walk over to the large window front of the lobby of the German Bundestag ... I am now standing at the window and can look directly over to Bellevue Palace. We see there that the president's limousines are parked in front of the entrance and also still waiting for Horst Koehler.«

In the meantime, an attentive colleague must have recognized Ulrich Deppendorf's dilemma and quickly organized an interview partner. A fine example of cooperation without many words.

»I'm going back to my reporter's desk now and I can see someone waiting there for me ...«

If we consciously look at this scene, it seems a bit silly at first sight, because the reporter did not report anything of substance. He only addressed what he was doing anyway. Nobody really cared. But probably hardly anyone noticed. If he had said helplessly: »I don't know what to do now either«, and had remained at his desk in silence, the spectators would have been irritated and the next day every tabloid would have reported about it blasphemously. This irritation was successfully avoided by his verbal maneuver. The brains of the audience felt the warm stream of words giving orientation and together they waited patiently for the appearance of the Federal President.

Well done, Ulrich.

Let's go back to the network event. This time we accompany a young man who wants to connect to a young woman. Going forth – Arriving – Going along – Taking along, this was the secret formula.

A modified version applies to private conversations: Going forth – Arriving – Going along – Going along – Going along – Moving on together.

Man:	»I came from back there and I'm standing here now.«
Woman:	»So what?«
Man:	»And you see me thinking about what to say now.«
Woman:	»Well, now I'm curious.«
Man:	»I noticed something. If I may address it …?«

Woman:	»Go ahead.«
Man:	»I see this sticker on your handbag. For animal welfare. I like that.«
Woman:	»Oh, yes.«
Man:	»And my guess is you're a very mindful person.«
Woman:	»That's right. Glad you see that.« [Here comes the first smile]

Addressing in connection with I-see-you signals must always be authentic. Especially in personal encounters, the smallest mistakes can have an unfavorable effect. The young man has made his own behavior transparent, has become visible and has addressed with the famous 4 phrases what he has perceived about the young woman. The smile at the end is his reward. Good communication means attentively accompanying the inner processes of the other person. Always start with the other person. Best start with an I-see-you sentence.

Wrong: »Hello, my name is Charles, I'm 45 years old, I come from Oklahoma and I love fishing.« Now the other person's brain is going to say: »So what?«

Many people act this way. It's a typical ego mistake. Why is this a mistake? Because the other person's scan is beeping now at the point »Does he see me or does he only see himself?«

That is why a good conversation always starts with an I-see-you-see sentence. Then wait for response. If you have perceived the right thing and found the right words, a yes-response will follow. Then you appreciate what you have perceived and take the initiative with a leading sentence, for example:

»I would like to know more about this«. You only take the initiative after you have built at least two contact bridgeheads. No leading without contact.

This is easy to understand if you look at it from the opposite perspective. A new manager enters the scene and contacts an order-oriented coworker, who has been working in the company for 20 years. He says:

»I'm your new boss. I'll take the lead now. I expect you to hang in. Okay?«

What the order-oriented employee thinks now, can be easily predicted. So, you start to become a mind reader. The better option is therefore:

Contact – Contact – Taking Initiative – Obtain Consent.

New Manager:	»Good afternoon, I am Justin Bergman, the new head of this department. I noticed, that you are one of the most experienced experts with a long seniority in our company.«
Employee:	»That's right.«
Manager:	»This is the first time you see me. And my impression is that you're wondering: 'Who is this man and what do I get from him?'«
Employee:	[Cannot suppress grinning]
Manager:	»Let me introduce myself. Okay?«
Employee:	»Sure, and I will tell you something about me.«

At the end always conclude with a closing question and obtain consent. A professional conversation always starts with a clear goal and an I-see-you sentence. And it always ends with a Yes. Actually, this applies for all somewhat serious conversations. The closing question is key. There are two reasons for this. First, this allows the other person to participate in the progress of the conversation. And second, this is a test. How far did I get? Does the other person want to continue the conversation? Now the other person may and must take a visible step forward, has to make a decision. This creates a genuine dialogue that is desired by both parties and creates commitment. This behavior is respectful and ensures self-esteem and dignity of the other. This is joining-forces-appropriate communication. The following example illustrates this in a particularly nice way:

In a noble coffee flagship store, which sells not only coffee but also exclusive tableware, there is a showcase with bowls in a peculiar shape. A customer stands in front of it, actually finds these bowls beautiful, but does not know what they are supposed to be good for. The saleswoman sees this and starts to move. One of those infamous moments. Actually, the customer does not want to be addressed at all. But now something magical happens:

Saleswoman:	»I see you're wondering.«
Customer:	[Turns to the saleswoman completely astonished] »This is true. Can you read minds?«
Saleswoman:	[Smiles but doesn't say anything]
Customer:	»I wonder what these bowls are good for.«
Saleswoman:	»I understand that.«
Customer:	»Do you know what these are good for?«
Saleswoman:	[Looks friendly at the customer] »No, I don't know that either. I wonder myself.«

Customer: [Baffled]
Saleswoman: »But they're beautiful, aren't they?«
Customer: »Yes, they are.«
Saleswoman: »What do you think? For what purpose could YOU use them?«
Customer: [Thinking] »I could prepare a dinner for my wife and serve the starters in them.«
Saleswoman: [Laughs wholeheartedly] »They're certainly not meant for that. But it's a great idea. Your wife will love you for that.«
Customer: »Okay, I'll take two of those.«

Why are these words so effective? The secret lies already in the first sentence. »I see you are wondering«. The perfect opening. Very complex. The lady let go of her revenue motivation. Instead she focused on the customer. She read his inner process precisely. How did she do it? How to read inner processes anyway? She saw him standing in front of the show case making a face. She took time to read his face. She interpreted what she saw. She found the right words and hit home. This is a perfect example of the above-mentioned transfer competence. To know where to look, to interpret what you see, to find the right words to address, to connect with the person behind the customer. A well set I-see-you opening allows the other person to feel recognized. He is mirrored and reflected in the other. This creates a special feeling of certainty, security and solidarity. At the same time, looking in an appreciative mirror allows the person to get in touch with himself and reflect on himself. An access to his own inner potential is created. If he sees something positive, he can further build up his self-esteem. If he recognizes something he does not like, he can sort it out in a self-referential way and successively start changing it. The verbal response is a linguistic mirror. It is not an invitation to do something and above all it is not an accusation or an appeal. By accusations or appeals we do not achieve self-reflection, but trigger resistance.

Wrong: »I see you're angry. Pull yourself
           together. Don't create such a mood
           here. You have to understand that.«

Right: »I see you're angry. I can only partly
           understand that. Tell me more about it.
           Okay?«

This allows for reproach-free self-reflection. Both conversation partners dissociate from stressful emotions. Both can now turn together and share the actual topic. The response creates inner distance. The force of the emotions decreases. Both can talk freely and clearly with each other again. The »wrong« variant is a so-called »mixed message«: I see you, but I don't like what I see; combined with the reproachful request that the other person should change. What is the probability that the other person will now say: »Thank you, now that you mention it, I realize it myself. Wait. I'll change myself immediately.«

Have you ever seen anyone changing voluntarily after being addressed with accusations or appeals? »You have to clean up your room. I told you a hundred times. You have to understand that.« Has this ever worked? In 99% of the cases, reproachful appeals for self-reflected acceptance with the request for changing behavior trigger spontaneous self-esteem-safeguarding resistance. This is not a addressing in an »I-see-you« way, but a demand. You can delete this from your language repertoire without substitution. You won't miss a thing. If you want to collect a claim, you can also use the 4-Phrase-Strategy.

»I see you're angry and unhappy.«
»Right.«
»By the way, I'm not the only one who can see that. Everybody does.«
»Really?«
»Yep.«
»Huh.«
»I can understand that.«
»Hm.«
»At the same time, we agreed that you only join the party, if you really wanted to do so.«
»Well, it's true, actually.«
»Good. Now, what are you going to do?«
»I could leave or pull myself together.«
»True. You could also do something else.«
»What?«
»You could choose to have fun.«
[Groaning. Agreement. Smile.]

The first sentence mirrors the other one without any reproach. The first sentence is clear and unambiguous when the other person immediately understands and feels what you are talking about. »I see you have a very special eye for detail. The choice of ingredients, the side dishes, it all worked out wonderfully. It seems to me you've given this a great deal of thought.«

Clarity does not arise when the question, »Was everything to your satisfaction?« is followed by the answer, »Well, everything's great.« At least, this answer does not meet the clarity requirements of an order-oriented person. But this also applies to any other type of personality. If you want to give recognition to a relationship person and say, »Hey, everything is great here«, then he is happy – for three seconds, but then he asks himself, »What is he talking about? Does he even mean me or is he talking to himself?« This is called a »Royal Visit«. A leader visits his subordinates, strides through the crowd, stops now and then, pats someone he doesn't even know and has never met before on the shoulder and says, »Well done, keep up the good work.« The person concerned is probably more embarrassed than flattered. You can imagine what he now thinks of this royal visitor.

The first sentence thus requires emotional clarity from the person who says it and must not have any hidden messages. The second phrase is also important because it reinforces the first and acknowledges and values the perceived. The third move takes the thematic lead and opens a fork in the road.

»At the same time, we agreed that you would only join the party, if you really wanted to do so.«

This is not a demand, not an accusation, not at all criticism, but only a factual statement. More is not necessary, because the person to whom the conversation is addressed usually knows himself what you are talking about. Self-reflection. What someone knows himself, one doesn't need to rub in. The other one already knows what's coming. He has to make a decision.

»Good. Now what are you going to do?«

This is neither an appeal nor an accusation. It is only a request to make a decision at this very moment. This is a deliberately opened fork in the road for the other. This makes the conversation serious. It creates a sense of urgency; but in a dignified way. The sentence, »Pull yourself together or go home«, on the other hand, can only be perceived as a kick in the butt and would intensify the already emerging conflict. If the other person would »pull himself together« and stay, he would humiliate and lower his self-esteem himself. Nobody can do that. Resistance would be the immediate reaction. Instead, he will most likely go into a confrontation with the critic, defend himself and fight against him, fight for honor and self-esteem. Such fights are relentless.

If self-reflection is successfully triggered through addressing in clear and respectful ways, the inner process of the dialogue partner changes. Now he retains the decision-making authority. If you make sure, that he cannot avoid the fork in the road, he will turn to his own inner process. He must face his own decision-making dilemma. Even now he has to fight.

But now he is no longer fighting with you, but fighting with himself.

At this point an inner space opens up for personal responsibility, self-value and strength. Here, what is experienced and reflected transforms into mental and emotional substance. The necessity to make decisions is no longer experienced as an externally determined intervention, but as an autonomous act of creative design. This is where unfoldment of potentials begins. Therein lies the importance and the impact of the fork in the road and the effect of the closing question.

The effect is based solely on the power of self-reflection. This is the deep source for reliable and creative connectedness and for intelligent joint action. Addressing triggers self-reflection. Thus, addressing becomes a magical tool.

Finally, we look again at Ronald and his resistance. Ronald has become a critical observer. You walk up to him, talk to him and he reacts with skeptical defense. Here too, the rule applies: The conversation always begins with the other person. It is not easy to follow this rule in such a situation. We perceive resistance as rejection, possibly even as an attack. And depending on our own personality structure, we react with retreat, defense or counterattack. To remain emotionally stable in such a situation and maintain focused attention to the other person is a special achievement. An extraordinary human deed.

But you can do it if you remember our proven strategy:

Observe – Address with 4 Phrases – Explore and Share.

1. I see you.
»Ronald, I see that you are very reserved and skeptical about me.«

Waiting for a yes. If you were precise in your perception, it will surely come. Maybe just in the form of a consenting hum-noise.

2. Appreciation, how this affects me.
»I find this surprising. I didn't expect this.«

3. Taking the lead.
»I'd like to know more about it. May I ask you a question?«

4. Closing question
»What is on your mind, right now?«

Ronald will now cautiously begin to communicate. Pay attention to keywords and signals, choose and pick the appropriate ones and explore [»Tell me more about it«] until his resistance decreases and a real dialogue unfolds. Sometimes you have to push a little bit.

You:	»Ronald, I would like you to accompany me to this network party.«
Ronald:	»I don't want to go to parties. Why is that supposed to be necessary?«
You:	»My impression is that you've made not quite so pleasant experiences with network parties.«
Ronald:	»Well, could be.«
You:	»Tell me more. Okay?«
Ronald:	»No, not okay. Why do I have to? You're just trying to sell me this networking thing.«
You:	»Ronald, today you make it really hard for me. You are a tough cookie.«
Ronald:	»Not just today.«
You:	»Right.«
Ronald:	»And now what?«
You:	»Well, what I notice is, that there is something really deep sitting inside of you. I would like to understand this better. That's why I'm asking. Is that

	okay?«
Ronald:	»Well ...«
You:	»Well? What do you mean with 'well'?«
Ronald:	»Well, that's actually okay.«
You:	»Good, then give me an idea what's on your mind. What are your thoughts?«

In this example, the key to dialogue is not to argue why a network party is useful, but to simply and solely address the resistance. Addressing triggers self-reflection. The inner process in which Ronald confronts his own resistance begins now. At first, he did fight against the party. Then he fought against you. Now he's fighting with himself. This is powerful, liberating, solution-oriented and above all dignified.

By the way, avoid asking an order person, »What do you FEEL right now?« When you ask him about his feelings, he thinks, »What do you care about my feelings? This is none of your business.« Sometimes he expressly says that, too. Ask for his thoughts. His reaction will then be different, rather positive: »The other one really seems to be interested in me.« This is due to the order preference. Thinking before feeling. It's different for relationship people. But here as well you should ask first, »What do you think?« And then you can move on to emotions and feelings. This is the safer way to reduce resistance or not to cause resistance in the first place.

We are constantly encountering resistance; with others and also within ourselves. Resistance prevents cooperation and thus the development of potential. Solving resistance is a challenge, a good deed and also necessary, because otherwise you cannot establish a real dialogue.

This leads to our roadmap for interactions with people:

- Setting a clear goal
- Who am I talking to?
  - Personality type
  - Degree of contact
  - Dialogue or defense
- Solving resistance
- Getting a YES for dialogue
- Leading a dialogue
- Exploring, sharing and exchanging
- Creating a »fork in the road« for a final agreement for joining forces
- Getting a reliable YES for joint action

14
The Wondrous World of Resistance

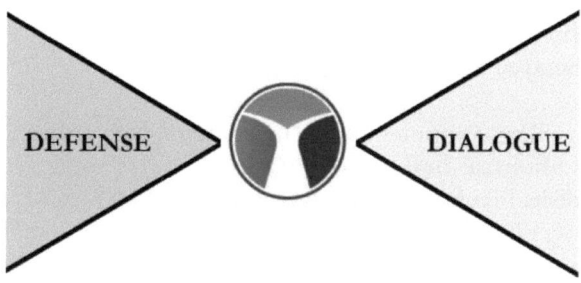

How do you create contact and interact with people who refuse to cooperate because they are in resistance or only pursue their own interests?

Do you know the Elk Cloner? This was the first known computer virus. It was written for the Apple II around 1982 by 15 years old US student Rich Skrenta. The virus was a boot sector virus and spread via the boot sector of infected floppy disks. If the computer was started from an infected floppy disk, the virus wrote itself into the memory, and as soon as uninfected floppy disks were inserted into the drive, the virus wrote itself to the floppy disks to spread further. With every 50th diskette insertion the following text appeared:

Elk Cloner:
The program with a personality

It will get on all your disks
It will infiltrate your chips
Yes, it's Cloner!
It will stick to you like glue
It will modify RAM too
Send in the Cloner!

The computer had to be restarted for further use. Otherwise nothing was damaged, only Apple DOS disks that were not based on the standard image were overwritten. The virus achieved great public awareness. Rich Skrenta later studied computer science and created a search engine.

This story shows that there is always someone who tests the limits. On one hand, this is one of those special capabilities of people without which they would not develop. On the other hand, they also use this ability against each other, being uncooperative and detrimental. How do people deal with this? People have a need for connection, security, order and orientation. The personality aspects relationship and order are expressed and reflected here on a higher collective level. People primarily try to achieve cooperation through friendly behavior and setting up rules at the same time. If these rules are violated, they will carefully check the root causes for the deviation.

There are people who simply do not understand these rules. As consequence you explain the whole thing to them again. Then there are people who simply cannot manage to follow rules. We try to help them with personal advice and support. In serious cases this leads to law enforcement, punishment and social rehabilitation.

And then there are those who deliberately break the rules or even fight them. This is where people run out of ideas. In earlier times they were simply taken out of reach. The English brought deviants to Australia from 1787 to 1868. Far away and never to be seen again. This is no longer possible today. Deep down, however, people still have the desire to be able to simply dispose of such deviants. However, again, this is not possible. Somebody is going to have to deal with them after all. People have not yet found a proper solution for this. Hence, people find themselves in a fundamental dilemma here. This is experienced as strain and stress. In the long run, positive perceptiveness and empathic sensitivity becomes over-sensitivity and people get highly strung with astonishing effects.

The Shock Denial Dynamic

It begins with an event that hits a person in one of his sensitive weak spots, the so called »Red Button«. If this event has a certain force and intensity, the person reacts with a shock. This is predictable behavior.

A passenger was sitting in an almost empty open coach of a highspeed train [»InterCityExpress«] from Hamburg to Frankfurt in Germany. He had his coat hung on a coat hook. This coat hook was placed between two rows of seats. In his coat was his wallet. In Göttingen another passenger got on board, chose the row of seats in front of our first passenger, hung his coat on the same hook over the already hanging coat and sat down. Our first passenger had a strange feeling, but his inner relationship part immediately appeased and calmed him down. When the train arrived in Kassel, the new passenger stood up, looked directly at our first passenger, took his coat and left.

This took a few seconds too long, so that our passenger became nervous. As a precaution, he reached into his coat pocket to look for his wallet. The coat pocket was empty.

What would a normal person do now? Running after the thief? This sounds plausible, but surprisingly, normal people do not do this. Our psychologically trained pickpocket must have known that.

For our passenger this was an event with sufficient force to shake up his inner stability. He suffered a moment of shock. Now it gets tricky. A person can only get a shock if he is hit at a sensitive spot. However, these inner areas are only sensitive if they have already been exposed to hurting experiences in the past and have never healed properly. If a person feels these spots, he is reminded of these past moments. This hurts tremendously. Now he wants to evade the pain. His brain therefore blocks out the perception of the acute event. This also switches off the pain, at least for a moment. The immediate thought that arises is: »This cannot be.« We call this reaction »denial«. This denial is a psychological splitting phenomenon. The human brain splits into two parallel realities. It KNOWS that something has happened and at the same time it FEELS something completely opposite. The brain is capable of this very astonishing reality distortion.

Instead of jumping up and running after the thief, our passenger actually thought: »My wallet must be somewhere.« And he began looking for it. Breast pocket inside right. Breast pocket inside left. Side pockets. Nothing. »Let me start over again, maybe I have missed something.« And then there's the briefcase. Maybe the wallet was not in the coat. That took a few precious seconds. Then the lightning of knowledge finally struck our passenger and he jumped up and ran to the door of the coach. He saw the thief already disappear at the end of the platform. At this moment the train conductor whistled and the doors closed. Too late. The short moment of delay due to the incipient denial prevented spontaneous persecution. A little later this feeling vanished into thin air and reality hit our passenger with full force. Whenever this happens, there is a final rebellion against the truth and especially against the inherent pain that is now inevitably felt. He became angry and furious. In anger and rage a person can still dissociate from pain for a few moments and pretend that none of this has anything to do with him. While a denial can last a lifetime, anger and rage are very authentic feelings, so called »primary feelings«. Such feelings don't last long. You can't stay angry all your life. Anger fades away after a while. Then a feeling of dejection arises. The person feels hurt, helpless and powerless. Now he is at a critical point in his inner process. Either he can't stand it and falls back into denial. Then a drama triangle with the coordinates Shock – Denial – Anger is created, from which the person will find it difficult to escape. Or he succeeds in taking the step towards self-reflection. He then feels his own responsibility, his dignity in the drama and he takes the reins of action into his own hands.

This inner process can be illustrated in the following curve. Horizontally you find the time line, the vertical line represents the perceived self-assurance.

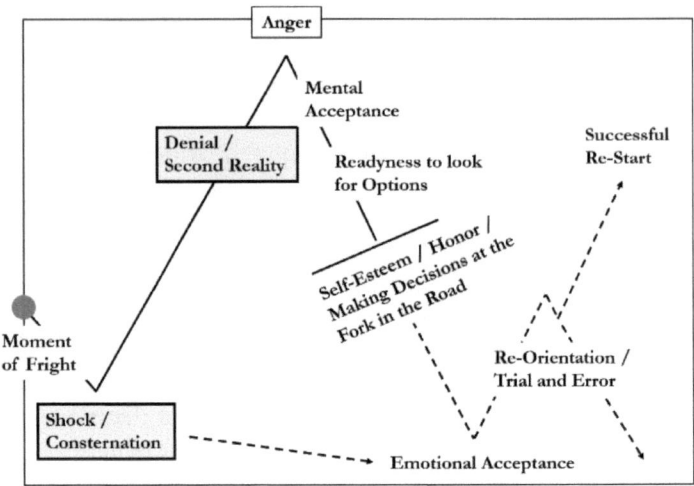

Our passenger went through this curve within a few minutes and then quickly wanted to call his bank and have his credit cards blocked. Unfortunately, between Göttingen and Kassel, that's why we emphasized these strange sounding German cities, there was a radio dead zone at this time. Our passenger was not able to do phone calls from the train.

The Shock Denial Curve started all over again:

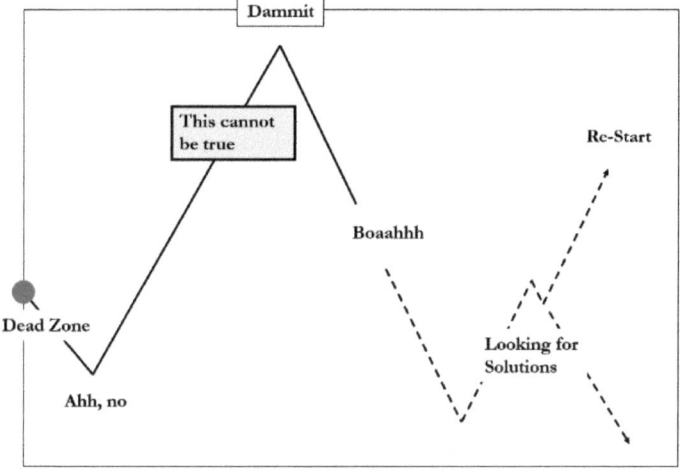

If this pickpocket had used his knowledge and skills to do a more meaningful job, he would certainly have had a successful career. But some people choose strange paths in life.

We've come full circle now. Adverse events can lead to denial. The person then behaves as if the event had not occurred. Some people dispose of their garbage in forests or dump it in the sea. The trash is then out of sight and out of mind. This is also a form of denial. However, people lack effective means to achieve a lasting, reliable and authentic cooperation with people who are unwilling to cooperate. This leaves people with unresolved fears and feelings of powerlessness, which leads to denial and resignation. Thus, people meet in different forms of individual denial. They communicate from one blind spot to another. Their behavior becomes ritualized and does not primarily

189

seek positive solutions but wants to avoid unpleasant and painful adversity. If you meet such a person, you can use our universal tool.

Observing + Sorting + Finding the Right Words + Addressing ▶ Self-Reflection ▶ Adjusting + Acting

In denial, a part of the self-perception is split off and deactivated. This also blocks self-reflection and thus, serious and intelligent action. If you are aware of this, you can start at exactly this point. What would you do as co-passenger who happened to be sitting next to our theft-suffering wallet-searching passenger and became aware of the situation? Now comes a multiple-choice task:

[1] I look the other way and mind my own business.
[2] I comfort the passenger and help him searching for his wallet.
3] I tell him very clearly that he has just been robbed and that he should raise alarm as fast as possible.
[4] I call the conductor and order two coffees and two brandies.

A resolution is probably not necessary.

We can now classify resistance as follows:

1] The most frequent resistance arises from violations of self-esteem, pride and honor. Our five personality types express this through their five fatal sentences with corresponding signals and behaviors.

2] Resistance results from blind spots and denial.

3] Resistance can also be based on the fact that people want to hide something and not let it come to light.

In all cases, self-reflection is at least partially deactivated. In order to overcome resistance and create genuine dialogue we have to get self-reflection going again. With the help of addressing this can be successfully accomplished. In simple terms: We hold up a friendly mirror. We do this by choosing the right words and clearly addressing what we see. In a certain way we externalize the blocked self-reflection of the other person. We do it for him by holding up the mirror.

Observing + Sorting + Finding the Right Words + Addressing ▶ Self-Reflection.

Examples: A relationship-oriented person feels inwardly disregarded and has defiantly withdrawn.

»My impression is you feel ignored.«
[Surprise]
»I'm sorry about that.«
[Astonishment]
»I'd like to understand this better.«
[Curiosity, first hope of relief]
»May I ask you what's on your mind?«
[Quick check, whether the person who is addressing is trustworthy]
»Is it okay that I'm asking this?«
If Yes, the conversation starts now.

An achiever personality feels devalued, has increased his speed, does more than necessary, wants to show it everybody and can no longer stop.

»Hey, I see how hard you work.«
»Yeah, right.«
»My impression is you want to show it to someone.«
[Surprise]
»Tell me, what's going on there? Okay?«
[Hesitation]
»You hesitate.«
»Yes.«
»I understand. It's not a common question.«
»Right.«
»Is it that you want to show ME something?«
»No, of course not. You have nothing to do with this.«
»Good, glad to hear that. You know, what I see is, you getting all worked up and wearing yourself out. That's what got me worried. That's why I am bringing it up. Is that okay?«

Most likely the achiever feels relief now and a conversation begins.

Our still searching passenger:

»Hey, you're still looking.«
»Yeah, sure. The wallet must be ...«
»Hold it. IT'S STOLEN.«
»Huh? You really think so?«
»HELLO. YOU'RE DREAMING. IT'S GONE. Get it back.«
»Really?«
»YES. RUN. NOW.«

This sounds a bit rough. But it's actually very friendly. Denial is not solved by a nice exchange of views. One solves denial by INTERRUPTING it. A phrase that almost always fits is: »My impression is, that you are not facing reality, but that you are deluding yourself.«

Another example: Gonzalez has transferred part of his duties to helpful Tanya and has not taken it back in due time. The reality is that these tasks have overwhelmed him. He is glad that Tanya is simply carrying on with the work and as a precaution he doesn't mention it. The »monkey« is doing very well with Tanya.

Tanya:	»Listen. Greetings from our monkey.«
Gonzalez:	»What are you talking about?«
Tanya:	»I took over some work from you. Out of helpfulness. Remember?«
Gonzalez:	»Yeah, sure. That was very nice of you.«
Tanya:	»Exactly. Helpfulness means helping. Helping out. For a certain time. Not forever.«
Gonzalez:	»Okay, I understand. Yeah, all right. Shall we talk about this next month? I'm drowning in work these days.«
Tanya:	»My impression is, I caught you cold right now.«
Gonzalez:	[Hums embarrassed but agreeing]
Tanya:	»I realize you know what we're talking about now.«
Gonzalez:	[Hums again]
Tanya:	»You are making noises.«
Gonzalez:	»Well. I understand. Yes.«
Tanya:	»I am glad. And that's why we are going to talk NOW about how we gonna get

	this monkey back to its own master, okay?«
Gonzalez:	»Yes, of course it's okay.«

This all sounds quite simple. These are also relatively »easy cases«, because the access to facing reality clearly and to create a moment of self-reflection is still there. However, it is not that easy, because of two facts:

- Tanya is forced to address something unpleasant, because of Gonzalez' inappropriate behavior. This is putting a burden on another person's shoulder.

- Now SHE has to deal with it, although it is HIS job. Frankly this is an unreasonable demand, an imposition.

- To make it worse, by being forced to taking action and addressing the matter, she RISKS to damage the relationship. For a relationship personality this is linked to her greatest fears.

Under such circumstance relationship-oriented people rather carry on the monkeys. That's why the above shown solution LOOKS easy, IS actually easy, and at the same time is emotionally very challenging. So, it is NOT EASY at all.

Now, if stressful situations in a person's life become more frequent, his denial reactions to them become rather chronic. This makes it more difficult to access one's own feelings and reduces the willingness to expose oneself to reality. The person is then partially no longer sensitive, empathy is partially deactivated. This blocks the inner process that ultimately leads to cooperation.

This is what we call a »difficult case«. But it is not the human being as such that is difficult. It is difficult to restore his inner sensitivity and ability to self-reflect. Not everyone is able to do that. Sometimes you need specialists for this. However, these specialists do not have additional secret instruments. They use the same tools that we have discussed so far. They just use them more accurately, more confidently and more courageously.

Imagine the following situation with Henry, the Territorial. He works as global key account manager, has created a broad network and uses this to his own advantage. Date and price agreements are not always transparent. He left the impression that he likes to plan visits to customers abroad, if he finds working in his home country too annoying or boring. Just recently he paid a visit to customers in Sao Paolo, Brazil. Nobody knew exactly why this was necessary. He makes independent decisions without informing his boss, the relationship and achievement-oriented Zigmond »Ziggy« Portnovsky. When asked, he smiles knowingly and says, »I know, not everyone can stand me.« His behavior is increasingly being criticized by others. He sometimes behaves roughly, rudely and dominantly. Many try to avoid him. Especially colleagues from inside sales have difficulties to compromise with him. They often argue about prices and delivery dates. Some customers also feel that he treats them inappropriately, are complaining about his casual and sometimes rude manner of speaking. Nevertheless, his results are good and his closing rate is high. Ziggy can't avoid a conversation. He tries his own way first and fails. Then he uses our tools. Both could look like this:

Ziggy:	»Hello Henry. Good afternoon. I have an issue today, that I would like to address.«
Henry:	[Smiles friendly]: »Of course, Ziggy. Always a pleasure. What burdens your heart?«
Ziggy:	»I'll be direct. You start stepping on people's toes.«
Henry:	[With an innocent face] »But Ziggy, I always do. You know that.«
Ziggy:	»Henry, please. This is serious.«
Henry:	»Listen, is there something wrong with my figures?«
Ziggy:	»No, of course not.«
Henry:	»Well then. It's because I can handle my customers. I know my business. And there's always someone whining. But they can't do it better.«
Ziggy:	»But then again, figures are not everything.«
Henry:	»What? This from you? Usually you are the revenue driver. Sitting on everyone's neck all the time.«
Ziggy:	»Yeah, but ...«
Henry:	»What 'Yeah, but'? Is it Mother's Day?«
Ziggy:	»Henry, really, seriously, you are giving some people a hard time. You make cooperation difficult for some. And joining forces in a pleasant manner is also a factor for us.«
Henry:	»Then they should directly come to me.«
Ziggy:	»Some people don't dare.«

Henry:	»Huuh, sissies.«
Ziggy:	»Man ... !«
Henry:	»What do you want from me now? Really. What exactly?«
Ziggy:	»I'd like you to be more conciliatory with internal sales.«
Henry:	»That must come from Jackson. He's always getting nervous so quickly.«
Ziggy:	»No, It's not Jackson alone, even customers find your behavior too direct sometimes.«
Henry:	»What? Who?«
Ziggy:	»I got this from someone in the Netherlands.«
Henry:	»The Hollies? Man. They're always so over-sensitive. I'm probably too German for them.«
Ziggy:	»And what did you do in Sao Paolo?«
Henry:	»Visiting customers. Pereira, Santos and Lugas. What's the point here? Are you trying to grill me?«
Ziggy:	»No, but you have to take a positive step towards people.«
Henry:	»Okay. I will. Is that it?«
Ziggy:	»Henry, really now!«
Henry:	»Man. Yes.«
Ziggy:	»Good.«

Quick check:
Did Ziggy have a clear goal? Rather not.
Was Ziggy able to overcome Henry's resistance? No.
Does Henry take his boss seriously? No.
Was there genuine dialogue? No.
Was there a reliable Yes at the end? No.
Ziggy should better try again.

Second try

Ziggy:	»Hello Henry. Good afternoon. I have an issue today, that I would like to address.«
Henry:	[Smiles friendly]: »Of course, Ziggy. Always a pleasure. What burdens your heart?«
Ziggy:	»I'll be direct. You start stepping on people's toes.«
Henry:	[With an innocent face] »But Ziggy, I always do. You know that.«
Ziggy:	»Henry, please. This is serious.«
Henry:	»Listen, is there something wrong with my figures?«
Ziggy:	»No, of course not.«
Henry:	»Well then. It's because I can handle my customers. I know my business. And there's always someone whining. But they can't do it better.«

Now, Ziggy changes the course of action.

Ziggy:	»You see, Henry?«
Henry:	»What?«
Ziggy:	»You do to me now, what you do to others.«
Henry:	»What?«
Ziggy:	»If someone enters your territory, you start shooting. Immediately.«
Henry:	»Uhm ... and?«
Ziggy:	»That's what in our culture is generally considered unfriendly and distancing. Setting unnecessary boundaries.«
Henry:	»Ziggy, you know me.«

Ziggy:	»Right. I know you. I tell you another thing. I appreciate you, too.«
Henry:	»And what comes next?«
Ziggy:	»You're a real battle-scarred warhorse.«
Henry:	[Trying to hide a smile]
Ziggy:	»And I think that's good. You are engaged and people respect you.«
Henry:	»And ...?«
Ziggy:	»And others are also committed and engaged and also deserve respect. Got it?«
Henry:	»Has anybody complained?«
Ziggy:	»Henry. What's the matter with you? What question is that? There is always someone complaining about you.«
Henry:	»What is it, that you want from me now?«
Ziggy:	»I want us BOTH to have a 'clean deal'. Nothing under the carpet. Open hands. All matters addressed clearly. All right? Are you in on this?«
Henry:	[Grumbles] »Everything open? Do you want to go to prison?«
Ziggy:	»You're such a tough nut. For everyone. You know what I mean? And that's why you and I are sitting here together and talk. Now.«
Henry:	[Grumbles again]
Ziggy:	»And now you're grumbling. You don't like it. I know that. Wouldn't suit me either. That we have in common.«
Henry:	»Where did you learn these phrases?«
Ziggy:	»Good, right? It works. You can see that, huh? Now you're speechless.«
Henry:	»I am never speechless.«

Ziggy:	»Good to hear. Then let's start talking. Are you in?«
Henry:	»We are talking all the time, already.«
Ziggy:	»No, we're not. I want something from you and you've been dodging the whole time. This is not a conversation. This is defense.«
Henry:	»What exactly do you want from me?«
Ziggy:	»I'll tell you that. But only if you are listening.«
Henry:	»Okay. Go ahead ...«
Ziggy:	»There are three things, that I noticed. First: You build up your own network and don't let anyone else look at your cards. Second, you alienate people with your very direct behavior. And third, I I get the impression, that if you feel annoyed you just hop on an airplane and visits customers somewhere in the world. Where it's just pleasant for you.«
Henry:	»That's really blatant, Ziggy.«
Ziggy:	»What? Henry?«
Henry:	»I'm one of the best salesmen around and you start treating me like a beginner.«
Ziggy:	»Henry, now you're distracting.«
Henry:	»What?«
Ziggy:	»You distract. This is not what we are talking about. The opposite is the case. You're a professional. In our league. on our field. And I want you to stay on our field. And I want you to pass the ball to other players as well. And not building your own fields, somewhere, in Brazil for example.«

Henry:	»These were important customers.«
Ziggy:	»I don't want to dwell in the details. This is something in general. I want – let me find the right words – I want you to be a co-player. Emphasis on »Co«. Got it? Now you.«
Henry:	»Ziggy, we know each other for a long time ...«
Ziggy:	»What's this all about, Henry? You are distracting again.»
Henry:	»What do you want then?«
Ziggy:	»Your Yes-Word. Loud and clear.«
Henry:	[Obviously struggles with himself]
Ziggy:	»I can see you are struggling with yourself.«
Henry:	»What do I get in return?«
Ziggy:	»That we keep on having fun together. Say YES!«
Henry:	»All right.«
Ziggy:	»You know what I want from you. Cooperative behavior internally and appropriate trust-building communication with customers. You are a seasoned sales pro. You know how it works. Is that okay? Even with the Hollies?«
Henry:	»Yes, it's okay.«
Ziggy:	»Is that a hundred percent yes?«
Henry:	»Yeees.«
Ziggy:	»Thank you, Henry.«

Quick check:
Did Ziggy have a clear goal? Yes.
Was Ziggy able to overcome the resistance of Henry? Yes, 90%.

Does Henry take his boss seriously now? Yes.
Was there a genuine dialogue? In the end, yes, 90%.
Was there a reliable yes-word at the end?
Yes, 90%.

Ziggy managed to come to terms with Henry. He is fighting with himself now. This fight is not over yet. But Ziggy has drawn a ticket to remind Henry any time and get him back on track. He'll probably have to repeat this, two or three times. Then Henry will align himself. At least until the next reminder. Overall, however, this is a good result.

Henry is not really a difficult case because his self-reflection is very much intact. He knows about himself, that he can be a challenge for others, he also adjusts himself when it seems necessary. As difficult cases, we judge situations with people whose self-reflection is seriously blocked and to whom we cannot find access easily. This, then, is the next step on our joint journey towards cooperation and unfoldment of potentials. We will look at such difficult situations in one of the next volumes of EDITION 99 with the title: The Situation Navigator.

Second Helping

How People Sort Their Interests

Successful interactions between people begin with observing, sorting and understanding. For this purpose, we have learned about five most important inner structures of personalities. Another interesting inner process is the way people sort their interests. There are five categories. Each individual prefers his own order of sequence. In most cases, there is a primary preference - the predominant one - and a secondary one. These five categories are:

- People
- Activities
- Objects
- Locations
- Information

Those who primarily sort their interests according to the category »people« usually have a strong relationship orientation. Connectedness, belonging and sharing with other people provide a secure framework, orientation and certainty. In the presence of similarly minded people, this type of personality feels comfortable and recognized. In such an environment he can develop freely.

Those who primarily sort their interests according to the category »activities« are more likely to be outgoing, extravert and action-oriented. In dynamic movement they feel connected with life and nature. They feel their energy, power and involvement, thus, feel alive. Mostly they want to share activities with others. Specific action is, however, in the foreground. The combinations »people/activities« and »activities/people« are most common.

Those who primarily sort their interests according to the category »objects« often have a pronounced aesthetic sensibility. For example, they might own a saxophone but don't play it. Nevertheless, it lies open in their living room and they enjoy watching it and having it around. For them, objects and things are not about possession but about internal references. Objects tell stories in which people feel involved. An example: Someone could own three bicycles and wants to buy a fourth one. You could ask him why he would do that, since he already has three. Then he'll look at you in amazement and answers, »I think it's beautiful.« This would not be crazy at all. It would mean inner involvement in stories that enrich and fulfill his life.

Someone who primarily sorts his interests according to the category »locations« experiences in particular spaces recollection and peace or energy and liveliness. Being surrounded by space, just being in space, without doing anything gives him a feeling of orientation, beingness and inspiration. Such places are often landscapes, libraries, museums, stadiums, streets, cities, squares or simply park benches. To be there is not to retreat, but to create. The room, the location, the space becomes a place of power.

People who primarily sort their interests according to the category »information« also experience orientation, belonging and inspiration. They are curious, want to understand, collect knowledge and therefore feel safe and comfortable in knowledge-based coordinates. At the same time, they like to share their knowledge with others and thus make a contribution. But only, if others bother to ask.

So, all are fulfilled, involved and connected in different ways. The sorting preferences can be heard in the language that a person chooses. An example: Here we have an achievement-oriented, extraverted and active person. He is mainly interested in activities and people. There we have a relationship-oriented, rather feeling and self-reflecting person, who is primarily interested in people and locations. Both have a day off, meet and ask each other how they want to spend the day.

The first one says: »I'm going to get my new race bike, call my buddy George and ask him to ride the 30 miles around Lake Greenwood with me [activities and people]. Do you want to join us?«

The other one [people and locations] answers: »I don't know. George I never really met. Race bike is too hectic for me. I'd rather invite Gina and Walt to ride the chairlift up Mount Goldendew with me and have a quiet chat at the restaurant on top.

»Oh no«, says the first one, »that's too boring for me.«

»And cycling is too hectic for me«, says the other one. »Well, have fun«, they both wish each other well and go their separate ways.

Who's right? Both. Are they coming together? No. It doesn't matter, you say. Right. Everybody keeps staying with what they love most.

Now watch the next scene. A couple. She is relationship-oriented, with an interest in people. He is achievement-oriented, with an interest in activities.

She: »I would like to meet Scott and Lucy today.«

He: »And what are we going to do with them?«

She: »You don't always have to do something. For me, I just want to see them again.«

He: »Seeing them again? And then what? There must be something we could somehow do.«

She: »You always want to do something. It is perfectly sufficient to just take the time and meet again, have a chat and enjoy ourselves.«

He: »Just meet them? Well, and then what?«

She: [Leaving the room with a groan]

Both situations illustrate the diverse and sensitive behavior of people. In the first case the two did not come together, tolerate this and peacefully pursue their own interests. In the second case, small differences in the subtle sequence of interests lead to disturbances in the relationship. In humans these two possibilities are very close together. A wrong signal and connections can quickly break down. This is especially true if there was not enough time and opportunity to get to know each other better.

When a »location« person goes somewhere, first thing he's doing is looking for a nice place to sit there. When someone asks him what he's doing, he replies:

»I am sitting here.«
»So?«
»I'm enjoying the moment.«
»And don't you want to do something?«
»Why? I'm doing something.«
»Well, you're sitting.«
»Exactly.«

For an activity driven person this is difficult to understand. A location person gains peace and strength from the space surrounding him. He can recollect and re-orientate himself. He draws inspiration and new energy. Kit Allowitz would say: »He sucks the marrow of the free space.« So, it's not like he's »doing nothing«. He's just not doing anything active on the outside right now. He shifts his attention to his inner world and is active there. If you want to connect, just address him like this: »If you don't mind, I'll just sit down myself and enjoy the moment." Then he would look at you in surprise and be happy.

Another interesting group of people, not so few actually, are those who are interested in objects and information. These we often call »collectors«. For example, they collect beer steins and are able to tell all sorts of stories about each mug.

There are also people who are interested in locations and information. They like to go on city trips and then partake in guided tours with hosts who are constantly talking and sharing information.

All of this is »normal«.

Actually, almost all people are »normal«.

Quick References

Perhaps you think it is difficult to observe and sort people so precisely. With a little practice, you will succeed. The reason: You have a high-class inner scan, which you can completely trust. And if you consciously use this scan from now on, it will become clearer, sharper and more reliable from day to day. The key to success is to pay attention, watch and listen. Here are a few pointed examples:

»Search for a seat«

O[rder]	»I beg you pardon, is this seat taken?«
R[elation]	»Huh, excuse me, hm, so sorry, I was wondering if I could still squeeze in?«
A[chiever]	»Doesn't matter, I can just stand.«
I[nnovation]	»Don't bother, I'll sit on the floor.«
T[erritory]	»Move, this' my seat.«

»May I have a word with you?«

O	»Of course, I'm just putting the cell phone on mute.«
R	»Yes, please take a seat. Would you like me to get you a coffee or something?«
A	»What? Why? Is it quick?«
I	»Sure, anytime.«
T	»What?«

»I need something from you real quick!«

O	»Wait please. I'm just going to finish this one and then we can concentrate on what you need.«
R	»Oh yes, of course. Sure. What is it, that's on your mind? How can I help?«
A	»Real quick is good. What is it?«
I	»Now I am curious.«
T	»I hear this three times a day.«

»I'd be interested to hear your opinion.«

O   »This honors me. What is it about?«
R   »Oh, that's nice. I am not so sure. I am not an expert.
       I hope that I can be of any assistance to you.«
A   »I'd love to, but can we do it later?«
I   »Do you have an interesting topic?«
T   »Do you want to kiss my ass?«

Once you have developed an initial assessment of your conversation partner's personality type, approach him in his own language, behavior and pace. He will then recognize himself in you and his scan will relax because of the perceived similarity. Here are a few tips:

O   Please choose a polite, not too direct way to address
       him. Keep a respectful social distance. Let your
       conversation partner set and structure the agenda.
       Speak moderately, not too fast and allow time for
       details.

R   Take time for personal topics, breathe calmly, stay
       relaxed. Share of yourself, but only after your
       conversation partner had enough time to share
       from himself. Don't rush. When time is ready,
       direct the conversation to topics that are important to
       you.

A   Don't beat around the bush. Get to the point quickly.
       Talk a little faster than usual. That's it already.

I   Share ideas. If you just don't have any, let yourself
       being inspired by your conversation partner. He will
       probably have lots of ideas to share. More is not
       necessary. And by no means inadvertently restrict his
       freedom.

T   Stand firm, do not wobble, do not appease,
     Hold your stand. Address him directly, don't be
     too polite, get down to business.

And now: Get ready to joining forces!

The Next Book

**The Situation Navigator –
How you always find the right paths to solutions in
complex management landscapes**
[Expected to be released May 2022]

**Part 1
The Search Engine**

Most people love search engines. A wealth of information
becomes accessible to them. They quickly find what they
need and get something very fundamental: orientation. The
daily interaction between people often leads to problematic
situations. They need solutions for this. In the complexity
of situations, however, people often lose the overview, do
not find the right strategy quickly enough and maneuver
themselves into dead ends. To avoid this there is this search
engine, the Situation Navigator.

Situations, in our understanding, are always interactions
between people. An example: You get stuck in a snowstorm
with your car. This is not a situation we are dealing with
here. However, if there is another passenger in your car,
who is moaning and complaining like, »I saw this coming,
but you didn't listen to me«, our search engine will start. To
make the use of the Situation Navigator as simple and
concrete as possible, we will first look at situations between
two people. Situations in which several people are involved
will follow in the further course of this book series. These
could be situations such as a dispute between members of
an association during a general assembly, leading teams
through crises, tensions in a triangular relationship or the
failed birthday party of a family of twelve. In order to
further simplify our start into situation navigation, we
primarily consider interactions between two people in the
world of labor. The colorful world of private interactions
follows later – situations such as applying for rental of an
apartment, trouble with a noisy neighbor, cell phone

providers who put you on hold, with the endlessly repeated phrase, »We care about your call«, or coughing, sniffing and loudly phoning people with whom you are cramped for hours on buses, trains or planes.

First of all, we focus on situations between two people in the business world. Here we also find a complex variety of situations. In the following we shall focus on one-on-one leadership situations.

The Situation Navigator at a glance.

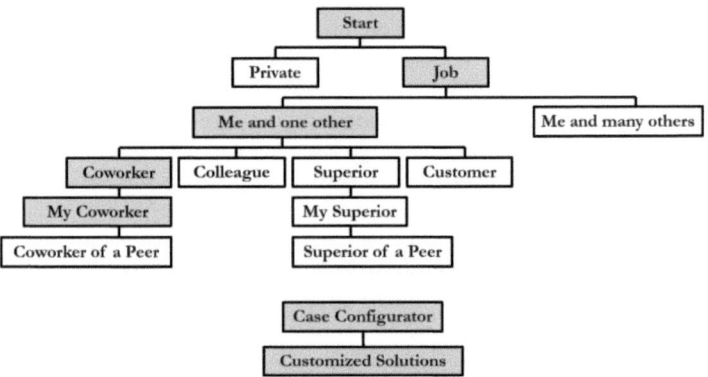

We follow this path: Start – Job – Me and one other – Coworker – My Coworker – Case Configurator – Customized Solutions.

You might now think that every situation is unique and a case configuration is not possible. Although there seems to be an immense number of different situations, on closer inspection you can see repetitions and patterns. We follow these patterns. The benefit for you is that this thought structure allows you to sort the complexity of cases and navigate more safely and clearly through the variety. Once you're on the right track, you can take a closer look at the individual details of each case situation.

01
Everyone Can Lead

The Situation Navigator is intended to serve both official leaders and the many unrecognized unofficial leaders. Everyone in a company will sooner or later work together with another colleague, exchange ideas, search for options, solve problems, make decisions and get something done together. Each of the parties involved thus creates a special performance process and tries to lead it to a positive solution, a decision and quick execution. This also is leadership. This unrecognized, unofficial managerial work will become increasingly important in the future. We are just saying goodbye to old management traditions, roles and hierarchies. This will no longer exist in the future. The old guys now twitch and say, »I don't believe that« and hold on to old thinking patterns and behaviors. But that's just an echo. The new generations have long since set out to rethink the ways people work together in organizations. And they will soon put this into practice.

The most current leadership ideas are: Self-referential competence assessments independent from benchmarking consultants, co-creation and self-supervision of teams, especially at interfaces. There are many different views and perspectives on this issue. It is being discussed whether managers will be required at all in the future. Some want to do without them, probably because of years of bad experience. The others are afraid of becoming obsolete. Self-organization is proclaimed as a goal. The amazing reality is that people have always been and will always be in a state of self-organization. Nature has not created leaders and followers. By nature, we are all equal in rank and initially without leadership. Thus, life is a gigantic experiment in self-organization and we find ourselves right in the middle of it. Self-organization is the basic principle of all human interaction. At the same time, a hierarchical order principle has become the preferred model: Heads of families – clan leaders – chiefs – captains – party leaders –

kings and queens – presidents – and ... managers.

That's not surprising. Self-organization is the inevitable consequence of a vacuum of order, structure and orientation. People usually experience mental and emotional vacuum states as confusing and unsettling. They then look for orientation and security. In the sense of cooperative self-organization, they should now co-create mutual orientation and security among themselves. But when disoriented and insecure people join together, the first thing that happens is that a disoriented and insecure collective is formed. This does not yet achieve anything. Now is the hour of the so-called alpha leaders. Dominant personalities experience vacuum not as unsettling, but as free territory. Without thinking about it, they just take it over. Everyone else watches, is perhaps outraged for a moment, then weighs their chances for rebellion, takes a step back, avoids, and in the end even feels relieved that now a »strong personality« is taking care of them. Psychoanalysts speak of a need for dependency [Otto F. Kernberg, Ideology, Conflict and Leadership in Groups and Organizations, Yale University Press, 1998]. At this moment hierarchies are created. On a realistic view, the hierarchical principle as an ordering model will continue to exist for a long time to come.

But what we will no longer endure are dominance hierarchies shaped by self-focused individuals. Autocrats are dying out. Click Youtube »Winterkorn Hyundai« and you know why. Winterkorn was the CEO of Volkswagen, who had to resign after the diesel affaire. On Youtube you see him visiting the Hyundai stand at the Frankfurt Automotive Trade Show in 2011. Four minutes, bad sound and in German. You won't understand anything. Just watch the body language.

What will fill this perceived vacuum in the future are cooperation hierarchies of intelligent experts. Every organized behavior of people requires ideas, options, solutions, decisions and the fastest possible execution into real actions and meaningful results. No one can do this alone. This is only possible through collaboration of people with different skills. There is, however, no way of stopping smart people. When they don't get the necessary space to express themselves, they will set up their own innovation-based organizations. At the same time, they leave nothing to chance – or to the well-intentioned commitment of not-so-smart minds. They will establish intelligent cooperation as a foundation for think tanking and execution, but only those personalities who are on the same level will participate in the innermost circles. This creates subordinate levels. Hierarchies, therefore, remain in place. After all, all those who work in such cooperative forms of organizations are always in contractual relationships and have to provide defined services. Ideally, they are involved in problem-solving and implementation processes in co-creative ways.

This creates new dynamics of order, in which roles are to be redesigned and connected in innovative ways. Dominant leadership skills are replaced by intelligent cooperation, which overcomes vertical thinking in hierarchical silos and unfolds horizontally across departmental boundaries. This is a constant balancing act and leads to special challenges for future »employees«. They must be able to cooperate in a self-organized manner at eye level, must legitimize themselves through competence, maintain their relevant network of relationships in a resilient manner, and be capable of constant negotiation [This idea follows the article »How to Lead Your Fellow Rainmakers«, Harvard Business Review, March-April 2019].

Education is becoming a decisive factor for the success of future organizational interaction processes. In addition to expert knowledge, this special education portfolio includes above all leadership and negotiation skills. Future »employees« must therefore become managers themselves. But in a new role. Parallel to that, existing managers will assume other roles. Their task will then mainly consist of protecting teams externally and internally and managing the interfaces. Self-organized teams often work in borderline areas. Unknown dangers lurk here. This requires clarity, honesty, transparency and a protective frame. There will then no longer be traditional managers and employees, but only experts who manage each other jointly. They will select colleagues for relevant management tasks, just as the Berlin Philharmonics choose their own conductors. And they will choose a different conductor for each piece. Self-organized teams are already working in this way today and call this »leading by competence«.

In addition to a new understanding of roles, what is necessary above all is complete transparency and the availability of management tools at all times for all those involved in the performance process. The Situation Navigator is designed to create this transparency. Everyone is needed. Everyone must be able to lead. Everyone is entitled to lead. Everyone can lead.

02
The Top Ten Leadership Situations

»If you make it here, you make it anywhere« –
Below you will find ten typical situations and a brainteaser. Classify these cases in order of difficulty:

- Easy
- Medium
- Difficult
- Worst Case

One more comment about the task. It is not about how difficult *you* find these cases *for yourself.* It could be that an inherently difficult case is quite easy for you to solve because of your experience. Conversely, a relatively simple case could also become a hurdle for you, because you have never dealt with such a case before. If everyone applied their own personal difficulty scale to situations, we would end up with as many assessment standards as there are managers. There would then be no reliable, transparent and ultimately fair and equally binding framework for assessing situations. And there would also be no clear line in the development and implementation of solutions. The consequence would be an uncoordinated arbitrary behavior of all parties involved. You therefore need general assessment criteria for the degree of difficulty of a situation regardless of your current personal problem-solving and leadership skills. Please try to define these criteria and then classify the case situations. We then look at the tools and skills needed to solve these cases safely and successfully.

Here are the ten cases now:

1. Tanya

... is 35 years old and works in order handling. The sales department has increased the sale of component products that have not been a high priority for a long time. The sales department wants to use these products as door openers. The deliveries of the individual components are coordinated by the logistics department, which is also supposed to inform Tanya so that she can trigger production on schedule. The responsible team leader in logistics, Gonzalez, is new in this role and still uncertain. A considerable backlog has formed. For the last three months he has not been able to do his job. Components were delivered to the warehouse without anyone knowing. As a result, production deadlines were not met. Customers are complaining. The sales department also complains, but not about the logistics department, but about Tanya. She has already spoken to Gonzalez, but without success. Tanya does not want to carry out this problem at the expense of the customers and continues to control parts of the logistics process herself. She checks the status of deliveries and thus ensures the assembly of the components. At the same time, she no longer fulfils her own tasks. She's making up for it with overtime. You are Tanya's superior, not Gonzalez'. You have noticed the situation and want to speak to Tanya.

The aim is that she will no longer take over the tasks of Gonzalez.

Easy – Medium – Difficult – Worst Case?

2. Ronald

... is 52 years old and has a lot of knowledge and experience. On one hand he is detail-oriented, delivers high quality and very good results and hardly anyone has more knowledge than he does. On the other hand, it is not easy to work with him because he is not very accessible, does not offer help to others voluntarily and expresses that he thinks some colleagues are not competent and committed enough to meet his standards. Ronald is now supposed to pass on his knowledge to two new colleagues, but does not do so and finds many arguments against it. He's aware of the fact, too. He knows that it is not easy for others to work with him. Nevertheless, he considers anyone unsuitable, who is not as conscientious and detail-oriented as he is. He does not feel obliged to share his knowledge and experience with these »uneducated people«. If someone wants to know something, they should ask. But they'd better ask the right questions. After all, he is not the trainer of these people. All this does not make working with him any easier. As his superior, it is important to you that Ronald shares his knowledge with his two new colleagues. You seek the conversation, but fear that he will refuse your request.

Easy – Medium – Difficult – Worst Case?

3. Susan

... is a successful and innovative employee, always full of good ideas. She is an engineer and is working on a special project for an important customer. The project has already been running for two years and Susan has visibly lost interest in it. However, the project is in its final phase and must be properly completed within the next three months. Until then, Susan's full commitment is still needed. New projects are already in the pipeline for the time after that. You as her manager have found out that she has already started a new project and is trying to optimize the »Turbostat ZX 3500«. But she hasn't been assigned to it from anyone. Especially not from you. You even were not informed at all. Your goal for her is to professionally complete the old project and then to permanently involve and dedicate herself in the following team processes.

Easy – Medium – Difficult – Worst Case?

4. Rudolph »Rudi«

... has solid expertise. He builds relationships and cooperates with others to get the job done quickly. He is confident but not self-centered. He likes to share his knowledge and reflects on his own and others' work in a way that is appreciated by everyone. He is always looking for opportunities to learn and improve. You can rely upon him even under pressure. Now he suddenly has a problem. His new girlfriend is starting her own business. She builds and sells surfboards in a shop on the beach. The business runs from Friday noon to Sunday evening. She expects Rudi to support her. During the last three Mondays Rudi was considerably late for work. You as his superior have noticed that. Since Rudi is a good and always reliable employee, he is embarrassed about this himself. However, he also expects your understanding and support. You take the first step and address the issue.

Easy – Medium – Difficult – Worst Case?

5. Daniel

... is 32 years old and works as a labor lawyer in the HR department. He is newly married, his wife is pregnant and both have just built a prefabricated house with loans. As a lawyer he is highly trained to analyze cases and provide detailed expert advice. His scope of duties has recently been expanded. He is now responsible for dealings with works councils and trade unions. In this context, he should prepare, negotiate and conclude labor agreements in his own responsibility. To do this, he needs to make strategic decisions and implement them with negotiating power. Daniel behaves recognizably insecure, but does not address this and instead pretends that everything is fine, »he just has a lot to do« and buries himself in files of ongoing labor court proceedings. The urgent works council issues are not making any progress. The works council is already complaining. You think it is time to talk to Daniel.

Easy – Medium – Difficult – Worst Case?

6. Herman

... has worked for many years as a senior engineer for development and production of high-quality measuring instruments. This also requires components from external suppliers, which are procured by the purchasing department. The responsible purchasing manager received specifications from Herman, obtained quotations and insisted on purchasing the most cost-effective products. Herman clearly rejected this and took over the procurement himself. He told the purchasing manager: »This is my territory. That's for me to decide. I know best what components we need. Stay out of this.« Over years, he has built up a broad network, also with suppliers, and he has now made use of it. Therefore, price agreements are not always transparent. Herman negotiated with suppliers and decided on certain products. He also negotiated the prices. The suppliers have properly contacted the purchasing department, as they are used to, to obtain order numbers. The purchasing manager was irritated by this and explained to the suppliers that they first had to negotiate with him. The suppliers are confused. Everyone's complaining. Herman often makes independent decisions without informing his manager. When asked, he smiles and says: »I know I'm a tough guy. I won't allow anybody to mess with my job. That's why I'm so successful.« His behavior is increasingly being criticized by others. He sometimes behaves roughly, rudely and dominantly. Many avoid him. Especially the purchasing department has difficulties to find compromises with him. Nevertheless, his results are good and the quality he delivers is reliably high. You as Herman's manager have heard about it and must act now. You can't avoid a conversation any longer.

Easy – Medium – Difficult – Worst Case?

7. Janina

... is a very effective employee. She is quick to the point, does not waste time and is always goal and result-oriented. Due to additional customer requirements and urgent deadlines Janina has come under pressure. You can clearly see stress signals. She becomes faster and faster, communicates with others less and less or in a way that nobody can follow her anymore. She's putting in overtime now. Her performance loses quality. This began four weeks ago and there is no end in sight. You are her manager. Your goal is for Janina to find the right pace and balance and to again cooperate with all parties involved in an appropriate manner.

Easy – Medium – Difficult – Worst Case?

8. Santosh

... has managed a marketing team for a year and is responsible for global brand strategy. He has to design this for five brands in seven countries. However, he is reluctant to make strategic decisions. This has created a vacuum for action. The respective country heads have begun to fill this vacuum with their own local strategies. To this end, they use substantial portions of the joint budget. Santosh comes to you regularly and asks for advice. At an inopportune and impatient moment, you told him that you trusted him, that he should think more entrepreneurially and show more determination. Since then, he has not contacted you as often. But he is also not making any progress with the brand strategy. You are afraid you hired the wrong person. In worst case, you would have to replace him, which would cost time and further delay the strategic work. You have to talk to him now, at the same time you do not want to make the situation worse.

Easy – Medium – Difficult – Worst Case?

9. Carl

... has been working in production for 24 years. He has health problems and an absenteeism rate of 30 days per year. He shows no motivation to support his colleagues or to develop himself. Overall, Carl's performance is just fair. When it comes to overtime, he always finds excuses. If you want to address him about this, he evades with threadbare explanations. You can't get a hold of him. It is like he keeps slipping through your fingers. But now you need him for urgent overtime on two consecutive Saturdays. You fear that he will refuse and entangle you in confusing excuses.

Easy – Medium – Difficult – Worst Case?

10. Mandy

... is 36 years old, started as development engineer and worked for the last three years in customer service. Six months ago, she transferred to your team, because you saw her potential and offered her the job. She is not integrated into the team and her performance does not meet expectations. Whereas she previously only processed incoming calls [Inbound], she now has to actively make outbound calls. It is intended to inform inactive customers and potential new customers about product developments and to initiate business. Mandy does not feel comfortable with her new job, because she does not want to be perceived as a »cold call sales agent«. You trust her to do the job and you see the additional task as enrichment for her job profile. In principle, she is neither a low performer nor unwilling. She still does her work as she used to and also goes to lunch with her old colleagues. Her performance is accordingly just fair and her new colleagues start to ignore her. There was already a conflict. Mandy had a customer on the phone who obviously misspoke the tone. Mandy reacted abruptly and ended the conversation angrily. A colleague saw this and wanted to give her some advice. She rebuked him that it was none of his business. Someone called her a bitch. But there are no witnesses. You have noticed the signals and are aware that you have to do something about it.

Easy – Medium – Difficult – Worst Case?

Please evaluate the degree of difficulty of these leadership situations and try to identify objective and distinguishable criteria for your classification.

[…]

Footnotes

[1] Gerald Hüther, Co-creativity and Community, Vandenhoeck & Ruprecht 2018.
- »No living system exists on its own. It is always connected with other forms of life and can only live and develop in the midst of others ...« [Page 66]
- »The only strategy that enables a continuous, unhindered and undisturbed development of the potentials created in a living system is the constant adjustment and readjustment of the relational patterns established within that system to changing conditions, maintaining as close and varied relationships with as many other and diverse living organisms as possible.«[Page 69]

[2] Humans scan other humans in 150 milliseconds. Kimberly D. Elsbach, Brilliant idea sell better, HBM December 2003.

3] Thomas Junker, Die Evolution des Menschen, C.H.Beck, 2nd edition 2008, pages 112 ff.

4] Joachim Bauer, Prinzip Menschlichkeit – Warum wir von Natur aus kooperieren, Hoffmann und Campe, 2006 and Psychologie heute, Oktober 2006.

[5] Michael Tomasello, Why we cooperate, The MIT Press, 2009

[6] Walter Mischel, The Marshmallow Test, Settlers, 2015.

7] On the development of this model:
The American psychologist Henry Murray [1893 - 1988] presented a personality theory based on so-called secondary needs in 1938, which was further developed in the 1970s by David C. McClelland [1917 - 1998]. Both taught at Harvard University. In his book »*The achieving society*« [1961] McClelland described three dominant needs as the basis of

human motivation: success [Achiever], power [Power] and affiliation [Affiliate]. His concepts were explored by Richard Bandler and Klaus Grochowiak in the context of the development of Neurolinguistic Programming [NLP] and integrated into short-term therapies. Manuel Jork and Jörg A. Petersdorf expanded this model in the 1990s to its current scope. On this basis, leadership programs were developed by Jork and Dr. Georg Michalik and have been implemented in Europe, the USA, Canada, Brazil, Chile, South Africa, India, China, Japan, Malaysia, Singapore, South Korea, Thailand, Vietnam and Australia. Marcus Kaliga, Predictive Human Interaction GmbH, has developed an online analysis for this model. Suzanne Johnson Vickberg and Kim Christfort have confirmed the model in essential parts, substantiated it scientifically and published it in the *Harvard Business Review, March - April 2017,* under the title »*The New Science of Teamwork*«.

8] Malcolm Gladwell, The Tipping Point, Back Bay Books, 2001, p. 196 ff., and various publications on the diffusion theory of Everett M. Rogers.

9] Andreas Brandhorst, Das Schiff, Piper Verlag, 2015 [Caution: Science Fiction].

[10] Foreword of Arnold Schwarzenegger, Tim Ferris, Tools of Titans – The Tactics, Routines and Habits of Billionaires, Icons and World-Class Performers, Vermilion, 2016.

Recommended Books and Articles

Reflecting yourself

Christopher Booker, The Seven Basic Plots - Why we tell stories, continuum, 2004 [Here you will get to know your personal home movie and how to continue writing the script. But you don't have to read the whole book. It is very long].

The New Science of Teamwork, HBR March – April 2017.

Cooperation

Gerald Hüther, Co-creativity and Community, Vandenhoeck & Ruprecht 2018. [If you don't know which book to start with, then take this one].

Robert Axelrod, The Evolution of Co-operation, Penguin Books, 1984.

Applying cool strategies

Dietrich Dörner, The Logic of Failure, Perseus Books, 1996 [The Bible for all complexity sufferers. A must for all strategic managers].

Tim Ferris, Tools of Titans – The Tactics, Routines and Habits of Billionaires, Icons and World-Class Performers, Vermilion, 2016.

Finding the right words

Carl R. Rogers, Barriers and Gateways to Communication, HBR July - August 1952, reprint HBR November - December 1991 [Tip for family constellation specialists: this is probably the first time that the phenomenon of systemic perception has been described].

Many Thanks

After 30 years of coaching and consulting there are so many amazing individuals who I was privileged to meet and to gain and share knowledge with. Together we mastered innumerous adventures. How can I ever thank them? The only way is to continue sharing.

There is a particular group of people with whom I am deeply connected in this ongoing journey of learning and unfolding. I would like to thank all those wonderful, committed, intelligent and friendly people from Endress+Hauser in the US and all over the world. Without you I would have never had the opportunity to literally drill the marrow out of the bone. To find out all those little details about the awesome inner dynamics of people. Never would I have found the right words to win them to joining forces to create this world according to our values. Jointly we made it happen. A huge Thank You to all of YOU.

About the Author

Manuel Jork was born in Berlin in 1955, studied law at the Free University of Berlin and worked as labor lawyer and HR manager in Berlin and Frankfurt am Main from 1982 to 2000. During these years he was certified as NLP Master and Consultant for System Dynamics. In 1990 he started working as consultant and coach. He navigates executives and negotiation professionals through challenging situations and is specialized in creating cooperation between different people. He focuses on interfaces in organizations. Amazing things happen here. They are crossroads where competencies and performance unfold or get lost. He combines labor law and psychotherapy with organizational and leadership development. Together with a Swiss company, he has developed an international leadership program which has been implemented worldwide. The communication methods presented here are applied there. They connect all cultures. He lives with his wife and dog in Northern Germany close to the Baltic Sea. Together they have three grown up children. He is a member of Mensa in Germany and of Professor Gerald Hüther's Academy for Unfoldment of Potentials.

Contact

For further information:
www.shortcut-academy.com
jork@jork.biz

For online analyses of the five
personality dynamics:

Outtakes

There is an unavoidable truth. We learn from experience, and therefore, we learn from mistakes. In our colorful life we constantly face failure. This is part of it, as well as the humor to take this with composure.

1. At a snack bar

Summer. Shopping Outlet. Long queues at a snack bar and a saleswoman who is visibly on her last nerve. She's grumpy and stressed. A customer finally comes up to buy a bottle of water.

Saleswoman: [Grumbles] »Next please.«
Customer: »I see you have a hard time, today.«
Saleswoman: [Surprise]
Customer: »Annoying, isn't it?«
Saleswoman: »Who are you? A social worker, or what?«
[Both break out in laughter.]

2. A couple

She is relationship-oriented with interest in people. He is performance-oriented with interest in activities.

She: »I would like to meet Scott and Lucy today.«
He: »And what are we going to do?«
She: »You don't always have to do something. I just want to see them again.«
He: »See them again? And then what? One needs to do something after all.«
She: »You always want to do something. Why isn't it enough just to take time and enjoy ourselves?«

He:	»You know, honey, what I'm realizing now is, that the relationship with Scott and Lucy is really important for you.«
She:	»Yes. Finally you realized that.«
He:	»My impression is that you're quite mad at me.«
She:	»Well, sometimes it's a bit complicated with us.«
He:	»You're right. I'm sorry about that.«
She:	[Surprised] »Wait a minute. What's going on here?«"
He:	»What?«
She:	»Hey, you are making fun of me now.«

[Both laugh out loud.]

3. Absenteeism interview in a company

HR Manager:	»Jerry, we need to talk about your absenteeism rate.«
Jerry:	»What about it?«
HR Manager:	»Well, it's too high. Let me show you the records …«
Jerry:	»I can't help it. When I'm sick, I'm sick. I'm not choosing to be sick.«
HR Manager:	»Jerry, be reasonable, we have to take a look …«
Jerry:	»We don't have to do nothing. I'm going to see my lawyer now. This is harassment. Just because I am a bit overweight and turning 55 next month …«
HR Manager:	»Jerry, I can see … Jerry … Oh Lord …«

[Jerry has left the office.]

4. Lay off interview in a company

| HR Manager: | »Linda, I have bad news for you. We need to end your employment.« |
| Linda: | [Starts crying and does not listen anymore.] |

HR Manager: »Linda … Linda … but this doesn't make it
better …«
[Linda continues crying.]

5. Another lay off interview

HR Manager: »George, I have a not so good news for you
…«
George: »Like with Linda? She is a mess. What have
you done to her? And now you try your
luck with me? No way …«
HR Manager: »George … George …«
[George has already left the room. The HR Manager buries
his head in his hands.]

6. Father and son

Ricky, 15 years old and flat out in puberty, sits in front of
his computer and plays games. It's been for hours already.
He's not doing his homework. School has already
complained.

Father: »Ricky, I see you sitting there in front of
your computer and …«
Ricky: [Turns casually on his modern office chair to
his father.]
»Dad, cut out this psycho crap.«
[And turns back to his computer.]

7. At the hot dog stand

Customer: »They look pretty pathetic for $ 4.80.
They're smaller and more expensive than
at Peggy's."
Saleswoman: »She doesn't pay that much rental fee as I
have to. I need to stand here until I drop,
even if nobody comes.«

Customer:	»Then you should have chosen another profession.«
Saleswoman:	»Why don't you go to Peggy, then?«
Customer:	»Good idea ...«
[Customer leaves.]	

8. At the pastry stand in the supermarket

The saleswoman just coughed and is now serving a customer.

Saleswoman:	»May I help you?«
Customer:	»Yes, huh, four buns ... wait a minute. You just coughed into your right hand and now you're touching my buns with it. I see that.«
Saleswoman:	»Excuse me?«
Customer:	»Coughing ... right hand ... buns ...«
Saleswoman:	»What?«
Customer:	»How about cleaning your hands and from now on coughing into the inside of your elbow?«
Saleswoman:	»What?«
Customer:	»Never mind ...«
[Customer leaves without buns.]	

8. At a hotel

A traveler stays in a small country inn near a large city. The country inn is managed by the owner. She picks up the guest from the parking lot and guides him correctly through the check-in process. Afterwards he knows that he is dealing with an order-oriented personality. She is accurate, polite, responsible, loves structure and clear procedures. The guest now knows that he can relax here, everything will be fine, he just has to behave properly. But what is proper behavior in this case?

Guest:	»Well, you're accurate.«
Lady:	»Yes?«
Guest:	»You sure do set the pace for your guests, huh?«
Lady:	»So, that everything has its order. Don't you like it?«
Guest:	»Yeah, yes, I guess. It's just a bit unusual.«
Lady:	»What are you? A free spirit?«
Guest:	»Yes. You got that right.«
Lady:	»Then you have come to the right place. Only through clarity and order can the mind freely unfold.«
Guest:	[Starts laughing.]
Lady:	[Also begins to laugh out loud.]